A Fifteenth-Century Courtesy Book
AND
Two Franciscan Rules

EARLY ENGLISH TEXT SOCIETY

Original Series, No. 148.

1914 (reprinted 1962).

PRICE 25*s*.

A Fifteenth-Century Courtesy Book

EDITED FROM THE MS. BY

R. W. CHAMBERS

AND

Two Fifteenth-Century Franciscan Rules

EDITED FROM THE MS. BY

WALTER W. SETON

Published for
THE EARLY ENGLISH TEXT SOCIETY
by the
OXFORD UNIVERSITY PRESS
LONDON   NEW YORK   TORONTO

OXFORD
UNIVERSITY PRESS

Great Clarendon Street, Oxford OX2 6DP
United Kingdom

Oxford University Press is a department of the University of Oxford.
It furthers the University's objective of excellence in research, scholarship,
and education by publishing worldwide. Oxford is a registered trade mark of
Oxford University Press in the UK and in certain other countries

© The Early English Text Society 1914

The moral rights of the authors have been asserted

Database right Oxford University Press (maker)

First Edition published in 1914
Reprinted 1962

All rights reserved. No part of this publication may be reproduced,
stored in a retrieval system, or transmitted, in any form or by any means,
without the prior permission in writing of Oxford University Press,
or as expressly permitted by law, or under terms agreed with the appropriate
reprographics rights organization. Enquiries concerning reproduction
outside the scope of the above should be sent to the Rights Department,
Oxford University Press, at the address above

You must not circulate this book in any other form
and you must impose this same condition on any acquirer

Published in the United States of America by Oxford University Press
198 Madison Avenue, New York, NY 10016, United States of America

British Library Cataloguing in Publication Data
Data available

Library of Congress Cataloging in Publication Data
Data available

Original Series, 148

ISBN 978-0-19-722148-8

TO

PROFESSOR ROBERT PRIEBSCH

October, 1914.

CONTENTS

	PAGE
A GENERALL RULE TO TECHE EUERY MAN THAT IS WILLYNGE FOR TO LERNE TO SERVE A LORDE OR MAYSTER IN EUERY THYNG TO HIS PLESURE	
Introduction	3
Text	11
Notes	18
Glossary	125
THE THIRDE ORDER OF SEYNT FRANCEYS, FOR THE BRETHREN AND SUSTERS OF THE ORDER OF PENITENTIS	
Introduction	25
Bibliography	41
Text	45
Notes	58
THE REWLE OF SUSTRIS MENOURESSES ENCLOSID	
Introduction	63
Bibliography	78
Text	81
Notes on the Rule of Sustris Menouresses	117
Notes on Appendix to Rule	120
Glossary for the Thirde Order and the Rewle of Sustris Menouresses enclosid	126

A Generall Rule
to teche euery man that is willynge
for to lerne, to serve a lorde or mayster
in euery thyng to his plesure

EDITED FROM A XVTH CENTURY MS.

IN THE BRITISH MUSEUM

(MS. Addl. 37969)

WITH AN

INTRODUCTION AND NOTES

BY

R. W. CHAMBERS, M.A., D.Lit.

INTRODUCTION

It is almost exactly four years since Dr. Furnivall, during his last illness, asked me to edit the first of the tracts in this volume. 'A month ago,' he wrote, 'Quaritch sent me a little 15th-century MS. of twelve pages (I think) on the duties of the Marshal and other officers of a big household. Thinking it interesting and unique, I sent it on to Dr. Warren, and he, agreeing, bought it for the British Museum.'

MS. Addl. 37969, as it now is, consists of nine leaves. It contains, besides this part detailing the duties of officials, various memoranda about wood carried partly at Talatun (? Talaton in Devon), some medical recipes in English and Latin, and a vellum fragment which was formerly in the binding, and contains some fifteenth-century accounts. But the only thing of much interest is the 'generall Rule to teche euery man that is willynge for to lerne to serve a lorde or mayster in euery thyng to his plesure'. So far as I can gather, Dr. Furnivall was right in describing this tract as unique; no other treatise seems to correspond to it closely in detail. But it is one of a very numerous class of which, in the opening years of the *Early English Text Society*, Dr. Furnivall made a special study. During the sixties he edited for the Society three volumes of Books of Courtesy, Books of Nurture, Books of Carving, Babies' Books, and other treatises illustrating English manners.

It was during the fifteenth century that this type of book flourished peculiarly in England: in other countries—in Italy and Provence—it is found much earlier. It has been stated that the early Italian courtesy books 'are few and of little mark'.[1] But probably there was a considerable body of Italian courtesy books which has been lost:[2] and, in any case, some early and important

[1] *Italian Courtesy Books in the Sixteenth Century*, by James W. Holme, in *Mod. Lang. Rev.*, v, 1910, p. 145.
[2] *Italian Courtesy Books*, by Jessie Crosland (*Mod. Lang. Rev.*, v, 502-4).

Italian books of manners have been preserved. Thomasin von Zirklaria, the author of the South German treatise *Der Wälsche Gast*, was an Italian. *Der Wälsche Gast*, though not essentially a courtesy book, contains the elements which go to make one. And Thomasin tells us that he had written in *welhschen* a book of courtesy, *buoch von der hüfscheit*.[2] Then there is Ser Brunetto Latini, who wrote much concerning courtesy in his *Tesoretto*, the little book in which he treated of all things appertaining to the human race.

Above all, long before any courtesy book appeared in English, whilst Dante was still a young man, 'Fra Bonvexino da Riva' wrote his *Zinquanta Cortexie da Tarola*, 'Fifty rules of courtesy for the table.' In many ways these rules remind us of the English courtesy books of two centuries later. Cats and dogs are not to be fondled at meals:

'The third rule after the thirtieth: not to stroke with the hands, so long as thou eatest at the table, either cat, or dog. It is not allowed unto the courteous to stroke animals with the hands with which he touches the dishes.'[3]

Compare this with the English rule:

    Where-sere þou sitt at mete in borde,
    Avoide þe cat at on bare word;
    For yf þou stroke cat oþer dogge,
    þou art lyke an ape teyʒed with a clogge.[4]

or

    Yf þy nown dogge þou scrape or clawe,
    þat is holden a vyse emong men knawe.[5]

or

    Pley þou not with a dogge ne ʒit with a cate
    Before þi better at þe tabull, ne be syde;
    For it is no curtasy—be þou sure of þat—
    In what place of crystendome þat þou dwelle or byde.[6]

---

[1] *Der Wälsche Gast*, ll. 1174 etc.

[2] By 'welsh' Thomasin probably means 'Italian' (see Schönbach, *Anfänge des Minnesanges*, 62) though his editor has interpreted the word as 'French' (*Der Wälsche Gast*, ed. Rückert, p. 531).

[3] La terza poxe la xxxª: no brancorar con le man,
    Tan fin tu mangi al descho, ni gate, ni can;
    No è lecito allo cortexe a brancorare li bruti
    Con le man, con le que el tocha li condugi.

[4] Sloane *Boke of Curtasye*, 105-8.

[5] Same, 87-8. But this second rule is a mistranslation of the Latin original.

[6] *Stans puer ad mensam*, 143-6 (MS. Ashmole, 61).

Introduction 5

Or again, take Bonvicino's rule that a man should keep silence whilst his companion is drinking, and not disturb him with questions.[1] With this compare the English *Urbanitatis*:

> Also when þou sest any man drynkyng
> That taketh hede of þy karpyng,
> Soone anon þou sece þy tale
> Wheþur he drynke wyne or Ale.[2]

or again:

> And if þou be in any place wer þi better is drynkyng,
> So þat þe coppe be at his hede, odour with ale or wyne,
> Doctour Paler seys þee þus, and byddes þee sey nothing,
> For brekyng of þi curtasy at syche a curtas tyme.[3]

If the drinker is a great man, good manners demanded that those near should refrain from eating and drinking, as well as from speaking. If your neighbour is a bishop, says Bonvicino, you must not eat[4] or raise your bowl[5] so long as he is drinking. Compare the English rule:

> And yif thi lord drynk at þat tyde,
> Drynk þou not, but hym abyde;
> Be it at Evyne, be it at noone,
> Drynk þou not tylle he haue done.[6]

Yet here we see an essential difference between the Italian and the English instructions. The Italian writer thinks of guests dining together: the Englishman is thinking of the demeanour due from a subordinate to his lord. This distinction does not hold good universally. Once, at any rate, Bonvicino speaks as if he were addressing those who serve.[7] But what is occasional in the Italian is almost universal in the English writers; they address youths who are supposed to be serving in the households of noblemen.

That a boy, instead of growing up at home, should be sent into some other house to learn manners, was, of course, an ancient

---

[1] Rule 37.
[2] ll. 61-64 (MS. *Cotton Calig.* A. ii.).
[3] *Stans puer ad mensam*, 235-8 (Ashmole, 61). Cf. *Babees Boke*, 92-3.
[4]   Mangiando apresso d'un vescho, tan fin ch'el beve dra copa
       Usanza drita prende: no mastegare dra bocha.
[5]   Chi fosse a provo d'un vescho, tan fin ch'el beverave,
       No di' levà lo sò napo, over ch'el vargarave.
[6] *The Lytylle Childrenes Lytil Boke*, 69-72.
[7] In his thirtieth and thirty-first rules, recommending the use of a pocket-handkerchief.

custom of chivalry. But it seems to have had greater vogue, and to have endured longer, in England than abroad. Young Thomas More served Cardinal Moreton as a page, notwithstanding the considerable distinction to which his father had attained; and Scott, in his essay on Chivalry, records a survival of this practice into the eighteenth century in the case of a 'gentleman bred a page in the family of the duchess of Buccleuch and Monmouth, who died during the reign of George III, a general officer in his Majesty's service'.[1] And, in the form of apprenticeship, this custom of sending boys away from home was as prevalent in England among the middle as among the upper classes. It aroused the hostile comment of foreigners, as is shown in an Italian account of English customs, written about the year 1500:

> The want of affection in the English is strongly manifested towards their children; for after having kept them at home till they arrive at the age of seven or nine years at the utmost, they put them out, both males and females, to hard service in the houses of other people, binding them generally for another seven or nine years. And these are called apprentices, and during that time they perform all the most menial offices; and few are born who are exempted from this fate, for every one, however rich he may be, sends away his children into the houses of others, whilst he, in return, receives those of strangers into his own. And on enquiring their reason for this severity, they answered that they did it in order that their children might learn better manners. But I, for my part, believe that they do it because they like to enjoy all their comforts themselves, and that they are better served by strangers than they would be by their own children. Besides which the English being great epicures, and very avaricious by nature, indulge in the most delicate fare themselves, and give their household the coarsest bread, and beer, and cold meat baked on Sunday for the week, which, however, they allow them in great abundance. If they had their own children at home, they would be obliged to give them the same food they make use of for themselves.[2]

The young man 'willing to learn', to whom the English book of manners is addressed, is accordingly assumed to be in the service of some lord: at the same time he is often himself assumed to be of good birth. Such books generally combine instructions as to deportment with practical hints as to serving.

Perhaps the most important of these books is the *Boke of Nurture* which goes under the name of John Russell. But the

[1] *Miscellaneous Prose Works*, 1834, vol. vi, p. 55.
[2] *A Relation of the Island of England*, trans. by C. A. Sneyd. London, 1847 (Camden Society).

Introduction 7

Sloane *Boke of Curtasye* is nearer akin to the 'Generall Rule' which is here printed: its first two sections give general instructions as to conduct and demeanour: in the third part the duties of the different officers are defined, in a manner which affords many close parallels to the 'Generall Rule'. And practical hints are given which bring vividly before us the picture of the page serving his lord, placing slices of bread under the hot dish to avoid burning his hands:

> Yf þo syluer dysshe wylle algate brenne,
> A sotelte I wylle þe kenne,
> Take þe bredde coruyn and lay by-twene,
> And kepe þe welle hit be not sene;
>   I teche hit for no curtayse
>   But for þyn ese.

A duller work, and more nearly parallel to the 'Generall Rule', is the treatise 'For to serve a lord'.[1]

But the closest parallel of all is to be found in a paper roll many yards in length, printed at some uncertain date in the sixteenth century. A copy of this is in the Bodleian, and no other is known.[2] This roll gives an account of the proceedings at the feasts held to celebrate the enthronization of George Neville as Archbishop of York, in 1466, and of William Warham as Archbishop of Canterbury, in 1504.

The Neville feast has been described as 'the greatest entertainment that ever subject made',[3] and some account of it is given in Godwin's *De Praesulibus Angliae*.[4] Earth, sea, and air appear to have been ransacked for victims of Neville's archiepiscopal hospitality. Of more common dishes, we read that there were served 4,000 woodcocks, 4,000 ducks, 4,000 pigeons, 4,000 rabbits, and 3,000 geese. But what makes this ecclesiastical gluttony of importance to us is the elaborate instruction as to the serving of the feast, which is appended. Nowhere else, so far as I am aware, is so

---

[1] Printed in the *Relation of the Island of England*, trans. by C. A. Sneyd, 1847 (Camden Society), and in Furnivall's *Early English Meals and Manners* (Early English Text Society), p. 349, &c.
[2] Reprinted (in part) in Hearne's *Lelandi Collectanea*, vol. vi, 1770, and in Warner's *Antiquitates culinariae*, 1791.
[3] Drake, *Eboracum*, London, 1736, p. 444.
[4] Cambridge, 1743, p. 695.

near a parallel to the 'Generall Rule' to be found. Most of the relevant passages I have quoted fully in the notes.

I have to thank Mr. John Hodgkin for having drawn my attention to this document; and Mrs. Crosland for valuable information, which I had overlooked, as to Spanish books of courtesy. And I ought to apologize for having been so long in carrying out so light a task. The delay enables this tract to be printed with two others, which, like it, throw that light upon the manner of life of our ancestors which always gave such keen joy to Dr. Furnivall.

The following books contain matter which illustrates the text printed here:

A Collection of Ordinances and Regulations for the Government of the Royal Household. London, printed for the Society of Antiquaries, 1790.

The Regulations and Establishment of the household of Henry Algernon Percy, the fifth earl of Northumberland, 1770.

Warner (Richard). *Antiquitates culinariae,* or curious tracts relating to the culinary affairs of the Old English. London, 1791.

Early English Meals and Manners. By J. F. Furnivall. London, 1868 (E.E.T.S.). [Contains, amongst other tracts, Russell's *Boke of Nurture,* the Sloane *Boke of Curtasye, The Babees Book, Urbanitatis, Stans Puer ad Mensam* (Lambeth MS.), *The Lytylle Childrenes Lytil Boke, For to serve a Lord.*]

Caxton's Book of Curtesye. Ed. by F. J. Furnivall. London, 1868 (E.E.T.S.).

A Book of Precedence, etc. Ed. by F. J. Furnivall. London, 1869 (E.E.T.S.).

J. Lelandi Collectanea, ed. T. Hearnius, Oxonii, 1715, Londini, 1770. 6 vols. [Contains the account of the Neville Feast.]

Henry of Aragon, Marquis of Villena. *Arte Cisoria, ó tratado del arte del cortar del cuchillo.* Madrid, 1766.

A GENERALL RULE

TO TECHE EUERY MAN TO SERVE A LORDE OR MAYSTER

A generall Rule to teche euery man that is willynge for to lerne to serue a lorde or mayster in euery thyng to his plesure.

The marshall in the mornyng ought to come into þe hall and se þat it be clene of all maner thyng þat may be fond vnhoneste þer In: þe stolis trestelles or elles formys yef ony be, þat þey be set in ther owne places at melis at þe bordes, and afore and aftur melis in corners farthest from encombraunce: and all þe hallynges and costers dressed in þer kynde places and shaken or betyn wyth Roddes yef nede be: and þat none houndes be abydyng in þe halle from morne to evyn. And to parforme þese thynges seyd afore he shall charge þe vsshere and þe grome of the hall þer wyth.

Also in wynter tyme þe seyd grome by þe ouersight of þe vssher shall bryng into þe hall as moche wode and colis as shall be spent dayle in the hall, and bere oute þe ashes and all oþer fylthe of þe hall. The seyd grome shall also kepe þe kay of þe woode and cole and delyuer it oute dayle by taill to | þe kechyn, halle and leuereys, [Fol. 2 b] and bryng the seyd taill to þe stywarde at þe wokes ende; þe seyd grome shall also contenually be in þe halle at þe firste mete or souper to bere away dysshes *and* kepe oute houndes and feche sawces *and* to obey all oþer commondmentes of þe hede offycers, þat is to sey of stywarde, marsha'l *and* vssher.

Also halfe an oure or þe lorde go to mete or souper þe marshall shall take þe Rodde in his hande *and commonde* þe panter and ewer to couer *and* make redy for þe lorde *and* for þe housold; *and* assone as it is made redy þe marshall shall commond the sewer to awayte when þe cokes be redye; and þen shall þe sewer go to þe ewry and take a towell vppon his shulder *and* þe marshall and he to go togeder and shewe afore the lorde, so þat he may knowe þer by when his mete is redy. And when it lyketh þe lorde to axe water þen shall þe esquyres *and* þe marshall and sewer goo by and by next þe lordis basyn and evyn at þe

lorde; þe sewer shall delyuer þe towell to þe worthyeste þat bethe
aboute hym and go streight to þe kechyn with all þe men þat shall
serue.

The marshall þen shall uncouer þe basyn yf it be coueryd and
5 holde it in his handes also vnto þe lord haue wesshe, and þen make
a salutacoun and take it to þe squyre þat brought it theder, and he
to bere it to þe ewry, and anone commonde water for all þem þat
[Fol. 3 a] shall sytte at þe lordes borde, and go wyth þe lorde to | be sette,
and þer asketh hym howe his bord shall be set.

10 And þe yemen and gromys or grome of þe chambre yef it be þer,
or the vsshere or gromes or grome yef it be þere, shall set vp bordes
and make redy þe stoles afore mete and haue hem redy at þe settyng
of bordes, and bryng hem redy to þe marshall when he callithe, and
also after mete bere away þe bordes, trestelles, and stolis; and when
15 þe lorde is set, and þe oþer bordes in his presence, the marshall shall
feche in his courses wyth þe sewer by and by; þe marshall and
sewer shall make a salutacoun when þey come allmoste at þe
borde, and none oþer þat berythe mete or drynke at þat tyme, to he
be delyuerd of þat þat he berythe.

20 And when all þe lordes messe is sewid, þen shall anoþer esquyre
next þe hande sewe þe oþer messes at the borde or in his presence.
And anone forthewyth þe amener shall bryng in þe almesse dyshe
with a loofe þer Inne and set it bynethe þe lordes salt or elles
vppon þe copborde yf no Rome be vppon þe borde; and a litill
25 afore þe seconde cours þe amener shall take of euery standarde or
grete mete that comys byfore þe lorde at þe first cours a sertayne,
wyth þe helpe of þe kerver, and put it in þe almes dysshe and send
þe voyde dysshes to þe kechyn. And all þis mene while þe
marshall shall loke bothe in þe chambre and halle þat þer lake
[Fol. 3 b] noþer bred, | ale, wyne ne mete þer as it ought to be seruyd, and þe
sewer shall loke þat þer lake no sawce in þe lordes presence.

And when þe second cours is redy, þe sewer shall come and warne
þe marshall, and þe marshall all esquyres and yemen waytors, to go
to þe kechyn. And lyke as þe marshall and sewer dyd at þe first
35 course so shall þey do at þe seconde; and when þe marshall seyth
tyme, þat is to say wythin iij quarters of an oure that þe laste
messe be sette in þe halle, the marshall shall commonde to take vpe
and all þe broke mete and broke brede to by cast into þe almes
vessell; and when it comyth to þe vsher yemen of þe chambre or

Ientilmen Then þe ewer to be þer, redy for to delyuere to þe grome of þe hall or mens seruantes waytors towelles for þem þat shall wesshe, and som men to be þer redy with voyders for to take vp trenchoures and broken breed, and assone as þey haue wesshe þat þe ewry be bore away *and* þe hall newe coueryd for þe latter mete. 5

And forthe wyth all, the amen*er* shall send for voyders for þe lord*es* borde, *and* all oþer bordes in his *pre*sence, and call all yemen of chambre *and* yemen waytors for to awayte vppon, and he shall take vp at þe lowest borde in þe same wyse that it was set downe, *and* so at all oþer bordes. And þe seyd yemen shall be redy at his 10 honde þ*er* to take at hym and bere þem to | þe kechyn. And when [Fol. 4 *a*] þe mete is vpe the amen*er* shall take þe voyders wyth þe trenchors *and* broken brede *and* þe clothe also *and* take it to one þat stondyth aboute hym for to bere it to þe almesse vessell. Then shall the amen*er* go to þe lord*es* borde and take of dyu*er*se met*es* as 15 it may goodly be forborne *and* augment þ*er* wyth þe almes dyshe, *and* all þis in þe lord*es* presence. And when it lykethe þe lorde to co*m*monde to take vpe, þe seyde yemen shall be redy þ*er* to awayte vppon þe amen*er* to do in all wyse as it is seyde afore. And forthe wyth all as þe seyd mete is vpe þe voyders to be set vppon þe 20 borde, þe laste afore þe lorde. All esquyres þen awaytynge to put in broken bred *and* trenchors or oþer mete, and þen þe amesse dyshe to be take away wyth a salutacou*n*, and set vp into a sure howse and after yevyn to one p*er*sone. Then shall þe amen*er* take vp frute yef ony be, and þe voyders aftur þe pant*er*, chese by it 25 selfe *and* forthe wyth aftur þe salt, hole bred, hole trenchors, kervynge knyves, sponys *and* napkyns toged*er*.

Then shall þe sewer, yf it be in a grete day and a durmant lye vnder þe clothe, let þe surnape with þe towell Rynne vppon the durmant. In a mene day festyuall þe surnape *and* towelles rynne 30 vppon þe borde. When þe clothe is take away In a symple day þe towelles only vppon þe clothe, when | it is made redy from cromys. [Fol. 4 *b*] At all tymes þe towell*es* to be dubble, yef þ*er* syt ony body byfore hym at his owne messe, *and* elles not. And yef þ*er* be a messe by-nethe hym *and* anoþ*er* above, Then þe seyd towelles to be leyd 35 sengill afore hym selfe and turnyd In ayen at eyþ*er* ende of þe table as ferre as þe p*er*sones sytte afore. And yef þe seyd towell be to shorte, þen þat þ*er* be ij short towelles to fullfille þ*er* defaut*es* bore in þe hand*es* of ij squyres or yemen of þe chambre or awayturs, *and* wheu þe surnape is leyde and þe esstate is made afore þe lorde, Then all þe esquyres to make a salutacou*n* at onys *and* go bake to þe ewry and *per* abyde to *graces* be seyd.

Then bryng in þe wat*er* in all wyse byfore þe lorde as þey dede
5 byfore mete, save þe towell. And yef *per* sytte at þe lord*es* messe one or moo ϸat be egall in esstate wyth þe lorde, þen make þe esstate byfore eche of þem, *and* bryng hem a basyn or basyns yef *per* be nede of mo þen one. *And* yef þer syt oþ*er per*sones at his messe þen of his esstate, þen let bryng a basyn or ell*es* basyns
10 vncou*er*yd and set afore hem when þe lord*es* basyns be set afore hym, and set þe ewer in þe mydd*es* of þe basyn till þe lorde hauc wesshe; *and* when þe lorde hathe weshe þen let þe squyre þat bryngyth thee basyn knele still till all þe borde hathe weshe, þen þe seyd esquyre shall bere the basyn to þe ewry *and* þe oþ*er* bas*y*ns
[Fol. 5 *a*] shall þen | folowe hym. And wyth oute ony tareyng þe copbord clothe *and* þe ewry shall be take away *and* anone þe surnape *and* towell*es* shall be strecchid; and þe marshall bygynnynge at þe lowere ende and after at þe higher ende shall bryng all þat leythe vppon þe borde byfore þe lorde and þ*er* take it vpe wyth a
20 salutacou*n*. Then shall be þ*er* redy yemen of þe chambre yef it be þ*er*, yemen waytors yef it be in þe hall, to take away stolis and bord*es* and trestell*es*, and set þem in þ*er* kynde plac*es*, and þe marshall shake þe lord*es* lape.

All suche poure, rule, *and* commondment*es* as þe marshall hade
25 at þe fyrst mete, whiles þe lorde sat, þe vsher shall haue at the seconde mete when þat þe marshall syttythe, wythouten þat it be count*er*maundid by þe stywarde or marshall.

Nota: as all these seyd s*er*vant*es* and offecers haue don at mete so to do at souper; and in þe same wyse þe seware þat stondyth shall
30 do as þe sewer þat knelythe except þe knelynge *and* þe assay. That is to say, he shall take the dyshes from þem þat bryngyth hem and vncou*er*e eu*ery* dyshe evyn byfore þe grettyst at þe borde, except potages *and* sawc*es* þat shall be set afore oþ*er per*sones, and cov*er*e hem ayen *and* set hem afterward in þ*er* kynde plac*es*, neu*er*
35 a dyshe above anoþ*er* and euer þat next þe lorde þat he shall assay
[Fol. 5 *b*] of firste aftur þe man*er* as it was sewid. And | þat none sawc*es* come In wyth þe courses except mustard, but aftur set in wyth þe sewer *and* esquyres wayters to eu*ery* mete as nedythe, or ell*es* all sawc*es* togeder afore the courses; *and* þat all esquyres waytors

or yemen yef esquyres lake be attendant in þe mele tymes vppon þe comondmentes of þe marshall in all thynges of þe kerver, in fechyng voyde dyshes or wyne for sawce of capons of þe sewer, in fechyng of sawce or all þat sawce shall be made of.

Also þat þe marshall sewer or esquyres wayters at mele tymes make honest chere wyth softe speche to straungers syttyng at þe lordes borde or in his presence, yef þey may goodly come to hem, and as þey se tyme. Also þat in þe lordes presence suche silence be kepte þat þer be no lowde speche save only of þe lorde and suche as he speketh to. And in þe hall suche lowe communecacoun be hade þat þe hede officers voyce be herde vnto all oþer offecers; and þat no gromys hede be coueryd seruyng at meles yeman, ne yeman Ientilman, ne Ientilman þe stywarde; also þat þe Ientilmen and yemen serue all þo in þe lordes presence; and oute of þe lordes presence yemen serue Ientilmen and set downe yemen and gromes serue hem, set gromes and pages to serue þem.

Then þe marshall in a lordes howse is Ientilman herberoure and þe vsher of þe hall yeman of þe same; and after þe vsher of thee chambre yef ony be, or yemen of þe chambre¹ in his absence haue [Fol. 6 a] take vpe logyng for his lorde and for hym selfe in his owne maner or in oþer places, þe marshall or þe vsshere in his stede shall assigne all oþer men þer logynges, as well strangers as men of housold; and also he shall assigne þem bred, ale, wyne, wex, talowe, and fewell to þer logynge after þe season of þe yere, and þer degrees, and rekyn for it dayle and wokely as þe lordes bookes be made.

Then þe marshall and vssher shall dayle reken all þe messes wythin þe howse, þat is to say þe lorde for ij messe and euery lorde in þe same wyse at þe borde; afturward euery man at þe borde for one messe, and þen aftur þroughe þe howse Ientilmen, yemen, gromes and pages euery ij to one messe; and in þe same wyse bryng hem dayle and wokely to þe clerke of þe kechyn as þey ben asked, and þe bokes made.

Also þe marshall hathe poure to correcte all suche as dothe grete offences wythin þe howse or wythoute, as in fightyng, oreble chydyng, makyng of debates, drawyng of knyves and stelynges, affrayes and suche oþer: to put hem into þe porters warde or in stokkes in all wyse as ferre forthe as þe stywarde, save in puttyng out of þe howse. And in all þese poyntes in lyke wyse þe vssher

¹ yef ony be *deleted*.

[Fol. 6 b] hathe þe same | powre in þe marshalles absence; all þis to be þus vnderstond, þe styward above all the Ientilmen, þe marshall above yemen, the vsher above gromes and pages.

Also at all tymes of þe day þe marshall shall haue his commond-
5 mentes fullfillid in euery office of þe house, and þe vsher in þe same wyse; to it be contermaundid, restrayned, or moderd by þe lord for þer waste or inportunyte.

Also at euery tyme þat þe lorde commondyth drynke, þe marshall or vssher shall warne esquyres or yemen to awayte þeron,
10 and þey shall goo wyth hym and commonde it at euery office; and In case þer be so many lordes and strangers þat þere shall nede pottes wyth wyne, þen shall þe marshall call euery lordes squyre or assigne oþer squyres of his owne lordes for hem, and þen delyuer coppis to þe seyd squy[r]es for þe seyd lordes, coueryd or vncoueryd, as þat þe
15 case requeryth at þe seler dore; and he hym selfe shall take as many coppis voyde eche wythin oþer by twix his handes wyth his rodde as he supposythe to serue þe remnant of þe howse, and so shall he goo afore; all þe oþer coppis, voyde save þe chef lordes, folow hym, and laste of all þe boteler wyth þe copborde clothe on his shulder and
20 pottes of wyne in his handes; and when þey come into þe place þer as þe lordes be, þe marshall, kerver, copberers shall make a saluta-
[Fol. 7 a] coun | and go streight to a bay wyndowe, a forme or copborde at þe lower ende of þe house yef ony be þer, and stond þer in order lyke as þey were delyuerd at þe seler dore, till þe coppis be fillid.
25 Then shall þe butler lay downe his copborde clothe and sette þe pottes þeron, and þe marshall all þe coppis þat he berythe in lyke wyse. Then shall þe marshall call þe squyres wyth the coppis, and do fell hem by order aftur þer esstates, and when all þe coppis be fillid he shall commonde hem to goo forthe to þe lordes, and forthe
30 wyth he shall call oþer Ientilmen or yemen of þe chambre or awayters and delyuer hem coppis suche as he brought, as many as he supposyth will serue þe house and tell hem where þey shall serue; and when þey haue all dronken þe marshall shall take ayen all þe coppis þat he brought hym selfe, puttyng þe wyne lefte in þem, yef
35 ony be, in a voyde potte of suche as þe botteler brought. And when he hathe ayen all þe seyd coppis, he shall take hem in lyke wyse as he brought hem, and þe boteler caste his clothe ayen vppon his shulder and take þe pottes in his handes, and forthwyth þe marshall shall geve awarnyng to þe kerver and copberers and

all togeder shall make a salutacoun and þerwyth departe, þe keruer first, þe copberers | next, þe marshall wyth þe coppis aftur þem, [Fol. 7 b] and laste of alle þe bottele wyth the pottes of wyne.

A generall Rule of all maner of fysshes, as þey shall be seruyd in order and course of sewynge.

The firste sprottes, rede heryng and whyte lyng, dogdrawght, grene fyshe, salt samon, salt elis, salt storgon and salt lamprey. 5
Then all maner of freyd metes, þat is freyd of salt fyshes or powderd; þen, folowynge þese fryed metes, all maner of see fysshe both rede, rounde and flat; and folowyng þem all reuer fyshe aftur as þey bethe of deynte and in gretnesse; and nexte folowynge all maner of pole fyshe and þen all maner of rostid fyshe, what so euer 10 þey bee; and þen folowyng all maner of shell fysshe; and folowyng þem all maner of bake metes, be it fishe or doucetes; lese þen ye haue many of þem þat ye lyst to departe som to þe firste course, som to þe seconde, and so to þe thyrde; and laste of all, all maner of leche metes and metes of deynte. 15

A generall Rule to euery Ientilman þat is a keruer to ony maner lorde.

The towell muste be layed vppon his shulder when he shall [Fol. 8 a] bryng his lorde brede, and yef he bryng frute his towell to be folden and leyd vppon his arme, what maner of frute so euer it be; and þe cause is þat þe towell ought to be spred vnder þe dyshe or pece or what so þat ye bryng it Inne; and euer yef þat þe esstate 20 þat ye serue stonde, þen aftur youre obeysance ye may stonde, and yef he sytte ye muste knele, and kepe þe dyshe or pece þat you bere in youre handes; etc.

Explicit a good techyng.

NOTES

p. 11, l. 9. *þe vsshere*] The duties of the Usher are explained in the *Neville* document:

First the Usher must see that the Hall be trymmed in euery poynt, and that the Cloth of estate be hanged in the Hall, and that foure Quyshions of estate be set in order vpon the Benche, beyng of fine Silke, or cloth of Gold, and that the hygh Table be set, with all other Boordes, and Cubberdes, Stooles and Chayres requisite within the Hall, and that a good fire be made.

p. 11, l. 10. *wynter tyme*] Wood was brought in from All Saints' Day to Candlemas Eve (Sloane *Boke of Curtasye*, 393-4).

p. 11, l. 21. *commonde þe panter and ewer to couer and make redy*] This is more fully described in the account of the *Neville Feast*:

Item, the Yeoman of the Ewrie must couer the hygh Table with all other Boordes and Cubberdes, and the Ewrie must be hanged, and a Bason of estate therevpon couered, with one Bason of assaye, and therevpon one Cup of assaye to take thassay therof, and thervpon to lay the chiefe napkin: and of the ryght syde of the Ewrie the Basons and Ewers for the rewarde, and of the left syde for the seconde messe.

Then the Panter must bryng foorth Salt, Bread, and Trenchers, with one brode and one narrow Knyfe, and one Spoone, and set the Salt right vnder the middest of the Cloth of estate, the Trenchers before the Salt, and the Bread before the Trenchers towardes the rewarde, properly wrapped in a napkyn, the brode knyfe poynt vnder the Bread, and the backe towardes the Salt, and the lesse Knyfe beneathe it towardes the rewarde, and the Spoone beneathe that towardes the rewarde, and all to be couered with a Couerpane of Diaper of fyne Sylke. The Surnappe must be properly layde towardes the Salt endlong the brode edge, by the handes of thaforenamed Yeoman of the Ewrie: and all other Boordes and Cubberdes must be made redy by the Yeoman of the Pantry, with Salt, Trenchers, and Bread.

Also at the Cubberde in lyke maner must the Panter make redy, with Salt, Bread, Trenchers, Napkyns, and Spoones, with one brode Knyfe for the rewarde. . . .

Then the Marshall with the Caruer must go towardes the hygh Table, and the Panter to folowe them, makyng their obeysance first in the middest of the Hall, and agayne before the hygh Dease: then the Marshall and the Panter must stande styll, and the Caruer must go to the Table, and there kneele on his knee, and then aryse with a good countenance, and properly take of the Couerpane of the Salt, and geue it to the Panter, which must stande styll.

Then the Caruer must remoue the Salt, and set it vnder the left edge of the cloth of estate towardes the seconde messe, and set your Bread beneath the Salt towardes the seconde messe, and let it remain styll wrapped.

Then with your brode Knyfe remoue your Trenchers all at once tofore the Salt, or towarde the rewarde, and then with your brode Knyfe properly vnclose the napkyn that the bread is in, and set the Bread all beneath the Salt towards the second messe: then the Table cleansed, the

Caruer must take with his brode Knyfe a litle of the vppermost Trencher, and geue it to the Panter to eate for thassay thereof, and of the Bread geue assay in lyke maner: then vncouer your Salt, and with a cornet of Breade touch it in four partes, and with your haude make a floryshe over it, and geue it the Panter to eate for thassaye therof, who goeth his way, then cleanse the Table cleane : that done, one Gentleman at the rewarde, and the Yeoman of the Ewrie at the seconde messe, must let downe the Surnappe from the Table.

Then with your brode Knyfe take one of the Trenchers stockes, and set it in your napkyns ende in your left hande, and take foure Trenchers, eche one after another, and lay them quadrant one besydes another before the Lordes seate, and lay there principal a lofe on them, then set downe your Trenchers, and take up your Bread with your brode knyfe, and cut therof three small peeces one after another, and lay them on the left hande of the Lorde, then cleanse the Table cleane.

p. 11, l. 24. *þen shall þe sewer go to þe ewry and take a towell vppon his shulder*] Cf. the *Neville Feast*:

That done, the Yeoman of the Ewrie shall arme the Caruer with one Towell from the left shoulder to vnder the ryght arme, and geue the napkyn of estate for thassay, and lay it vpon the same shoulder of the Caruer, and the Caruers owne napkyn vpon his left arme, and in lyke maner he shall arme the Sewer with an other Towell, from the ryght shoulder to vnder the ryght arme.

p. 12. l. 5. The washing ceremony is more fully described in the account of the *Neville Feast* thus :

In the meane time the Yeoman of the Ewrie kysseth the Towell of estate, and layeth it on the Marshal's left shoulder, and he taketh the assay of the water, and geueth the Cupbearer the bason of estate, with the Cup of assay. Then the Marshall with the Cupbearer goeth to the Lorde, and there maketh their obeysaunce. Then the Marshall kysseth the Towell for his assay, and so layeth it on the left shoulder of the Lorde of the house, or maister of the same, yf any such be, and the same Lorde or maister standeth on the left hande of the Baron bishop. Then the Marshall taketh the Cup of assay, & the Cupbearer putteth foorth water into the sayde Cup, and drynketh it for the assay therof, then he powreth forth water into the sayde Cup, and drynketh it, &c. and then powreth foorth water out of the Bason of estate, into the Bason of assay. Then the Lorde or maister of the house doth geue the Towel ende to the cheefe dignitie or prebendarie, to holde tyll the Bishop have washed, and then all other do washe in their degree in Basons prepared for them.

p. 12, l. 16. *þe marshall and sewer shall make a salutacoun*] This is described more fully in the *Neville Feast*:

When all is in course, the Marshall and the Sewer goeth together before the course to the hygh Table, makyng their obeysaunce in the myddest of the Hall euen before the hygh Table. Then the Marshall standeth styll, and the Sewer kneeleth on his knee besydes the Caruer, who receueth euery dyshe in course of kynde, and vncouereth them.

p. 12, l. 22. *þe amener shall bryng in þe almesse dyshe with a loofe þer Inne*] Cf. *Neville Feast*:

The Chaplyn must take the almes dyshe at the Cubborde, and bryng it before the boorde, and take the lofe of breade that standeth vpon the almes dyshe, and set it vpon the trencher that lyeth vpon the boorde, and then take the trencher and the lofe together, and set them vpon the almes dyshe, and with a good countenaunce take vp the dyshe, and delyuer to the Almner, and so depart.

For the office of the Almoner cf. also Sloane *Boke of Curtasye*, 729-48.

p. 12, l. 30. *þe sewer shall loke þat þer lake no sawce in þe lordes presence*] Cf. *Neville Feast* : 'The sewer must see that there want no sawces for any dyshe in his kynde.'

p. 13, l. 4. *trenchoures and broken breed*] The trenchers are therefore still of bread, not of wood. In the tract *For to serve a lord*, mention is made of 'Trenchours of tree or brede'. In [John Russell's] *Boke of Nurture*, of the early fifteenth century, the trenchers are of bread, 'a loofe of trenchurs'; and as late as 1465 the trenchers were clearly of bread at the *Neville* banquet, for 'cornetts of trenchers' were tasted by the assayer.

p. 13, l. 29. For the bringing in of the towels at the end of the Banquet, cf. the *Neville Feast* : at the close of dinner, after the wine is brought in :

Then the Sewer bryngeth the double Towell to thende of the rewarde upon both his armes, with an obeysaunce, and kysseth it for his assay, and then the Marshall commeth before the Lorde, makyng his obeysaunce. Then the Sewer layeth downe the Towell upon the Table, and geueth thende therof to one Gentleman, and so from one to another tyll it be conveyed to the Marshall. Then the Marshall must properly unclose thende of the Towell, and spreade it playne in the myddle of the Table before the Lorde : that done, he must have a rodde in his hande lyke unto an arrow stele, three quarters long, with a needle in the ende, puttyng the sharpe ende therof under the Towell, through the farre syde, holdyng the nearer syde to the rodde with his thombe, and also holdyng the end of the Towell towardes the Lorde for the estate therof, then make your obeysaunce, and geve the same ende to an other Gentleman towardes the second messe.

Then the Sewer at one ende, and a Gentleman at thother ende, to pull the chiefe Towell harde and strayght. Then laye over the one Towell towardes the neather syde of the boorde, and pull the chiefe Towell harde and strayght. Then the Marshall must put the sharpe ende of his rodde under the chiefe Towell agaynst the Lordes ryght hande, and therewithall take hold of the farre side of the Towell, and holde fast the neare syde to the rodde with your thombe, and drawe the Towell halfe a yarde forwarde the rewarde, and lay the bought backewarde for the estate therof towardes the rewarde, and after that an other of estate in lyke maner towardes the seconde messe. Then with thende of your rodde take up the narowe syde of the Towell, and lay it forwarde one hande brode, and stroke it over with your rodde from the estate to the other. Then laye the seconde Towell strayte wynyng it to that other Towell of estate, and so make your obeysaunce all and depart, and stande in the mydwarde of the Hall.

p. 13, l. 29. For the laying of the surnape, elaborate instructions are given in the Articles ordained by King Henry VII for the regulation of his household (*Ordinances and Regulations*, 119 : the whole passage is quoted in *Early English Meals and Manners*, p. 92); instructions are also given in Russell's *Boke of Nurture*, 237. In the *Liber Niger domus* of King Edward IV it is ordained that the 'usher of the chambre' 'maketh his towell or surnape, as dothe a Marchall when the King is in the hall': 'if the Kinge kepe estate in his chambyr, these ushers make the estate in the surnape, like as the marchall doth in the hall' (*Ordinances and Regulations*, 34, 38).

Notes on A generall Rule 21

p. 14, l. 4. *Then bryng in þe water*] Cf. *Neville Feast*:

That done, the Lordes Cupbearer, with other Cupbearers, do bryng in water, and the Lordes Cupbearer taketh assay as he did before dyner, and so setteth downe the Bason of assay, and putteth foorth Water of the Bason of estate before the Lorde. Then every man washeth at the rewarde and seconde messe, and at the Church boorde, and dryeth. Then the Sewer and Gentleman wayter draweth the Towel as they dyd before the washyng, and the Marshall maketh his estate as he dyd before the washyng. That done, the Cupbearer bryngeth in Ale, the Lord hath his assay, *ut supra*, and drynketh sytting, and al others, then do they aryse, and ever the better the latter, and the Lord last of all.

Then the Yeoman of the Ewrie must take up the Table cloth, the Usher must see the table, chayres and stooles taken away in order. Then the Lorde must drynke Wyne standyng, and all other in lyke maner, and that done, every man departeth at his good pleasure.

p. 14, l. 30. For the custom of taking the Assay, cf. the following passage from the *Neville Feast*:

In the meane tyme [i.e. while the guests are seating themselves] the Sewer goeth to the dresser, and there taketh assay of every dyshe, and doth geue it to the Stewarde and the Cooke to eate of all Porreges, Mustarde, and other sawces. He taketh the assay with *cornetts of trenchers* bread of his owne cuttyng, and that is thus: He taketh a cornet of bread in his hande, and toucheth three partes of the dyshe, and maketh a florishe ouer it, and geueth it to the aforenamed persons to eate, and of every stewed meate, rosted, boylde, or broyled, beyng fyshe or fleshe, he cutteth a litle thereof, &c. And yf it be baked meate closed, vnclose it, and take assay therof as ye do of sawces, and that is with cornettes of breade, and so with all other meates, as Custardes, Tartes, and Gelly, with other such lyke. The ministers of the Churche doth after the olde custome, in syngyng of some proper or godly Caroll....

And again, when the dishes are brought to the High Table and uncovered by the Carver:

Then the Caruer of all potages and sawces taketh assay with a cornet of trencher bread of his owne cuttyng, he toucheth three partes of the dishe, and maketh a florishe ouer it, and geueth it to the Sewer, and to hym that beareth the dyshe, who kneeleth in lyke maner, to eate for the assay therof. Then of your stewed meates, broylde, fryed, or rost meates, be it fyshe or fleshe, take assay therof at the myd syde with your brode Knyfe, and geue it to the Sewer, and to the bearer of the dyshe: and yf it be any maner of fowle, take the assay therof at the outsyde of the thygh or wynge: and if it be any baked meate that is closed, vncouer hym, and take assaye therof with cornettes dypt into the grauy, and geue it to the Sewer, *vt supra*. And of all Custardes, Tartes, Marchpaynes, or Gelly, take thassay with cornettes. And of all Suttleties or Leches, with your brode knyfe cut a litle of, and geue it to the Sewer and Bearer, *vt supra*.

And when the last dyshe of the first course is set in, the Sewer goeth to the dresser, and as he dyd at the first course, so he must at the seconde course in euery poynt, as touchyng the assay with other thynges, and when he is redy the ministers of the Churche do syng solemnly.

p. 15, l. 17. *Then þe marshall in a lordes howse is Ientilman herberoure*] Cf. Sloane *Boke of Curtasye*, 427–8.

The marshalle shalle herber alle men in fere,
That ben of court of any mestere.

p. 15, l. 33. *þe marshall ha'þe powre to correcte*] For the marshall's power to correct, cf. Sloane *Boke of Curtasye*, 379, &c. :

> Now of marschalle of halle wylle I spelle
> And what falle to hys offyce now wylle y telle;
> In absence of stuarde he shalle arest
> Who so euer is rebelle in court or fest;
> ȝomon-vsshere, and grome also,
> Vndur hym ar þes two . . .

p. 16, l. 8. For the serving of drink, cf. the *Neville Feast*:

> In the meane tyme the Marshall goeth to the Buttery, to see the couered Cup be right serued, and geueth to the Butler his assay, and delyuereth to the Cupbearer the Cup of estate, and when the Cupbearer commeth to the Table, after his obeysaunce, he kneeleth on his knee, and putteth foorth three or foure droppes of Ale into the insyde of the couer of the Cuppe, and suppes it of for his assay. Then he settes the Cup besydes the Lorde and couereth it, and then all the Table is serued with Ale. Marke when the first rost meate beyng fyshe or fleshe is broken, then the Cupbearer goeth to the Seller, and when the Cupbearer commeth to the Table, he vseth hym selfe as afore, &c.

p. 17, l. 12. *Doucetes*] Recipes for the making of these will be found in MS. Harl. 279 (see *Early English Meals and Manners*, 146), and in the *Fifteenth Century Cookery Books*, edited by Austin for the E. E. T. S.

The Thirde Order of Seynt Franceys for the Brethren and Susters of the Order of Penitentis.

EDITED FROM A XV CENTURY MS.
FORMERLY IN THE PENNANT COLLECTION

WITH AN

INTRODUCTION, NOTES, AND GLOSSARY

BY

WALTER W. SETON, M.A.

INTRODUCTION

THE THIRD ORDER

THE Rule of the Third Order, or Ordo de Poenitentia, as well as the history of the origin of that Order, is one of the subjects upon which criticism has been directed from the time, rather more than thirty years ago, when a serious study of Franciscan sources began. As in the case of so many other mediaeval problems, the not very extensive basis of ascertained facts and documents is liable in process of time to become overlaid and even concealed by the mass of theory and commentary which has been built upon such a basis. And yet there has not appeared in English a summary, first of the facts and documents which lie outside the region of doubt, and secondly of the criticism to which they have been subjected. As a Middle English version of the Rule is published here for the first time, it appears not unsuitable that an attempt should be made to provide such a summary.

Before, then, anything in the way of criticism or commentary is stated, it will be well to set out what are the actual materials and what facts are known about them.

1. In 1901 M. Paul Sabatier discovered in the Franciscan Monastery of S. John of Capestrano in the Abruzzi, in a fifteenth-century MS., a version of a Rule of the Third Order, having the following title:

Memoriale propositi fratrum et sororum de Poenitentia in domibus propriis existentium inceptum anno Domini M°CC°XXI tempore domini Gregorii noni Papae XIII° Cal. Iunii indictione prima tale est.

Whatever differences of view there may be as to this document in detail, all agree in regarding it as the earliest version of the Rule at present known. The full text will be found in Sabatier, *Opuscules de Critique historique*, Paris, 1901; and in Boehmer's *Analekten zur Geschichte des Franciscus von Assisi*. Tübingen, 1904. This version, which consists of thirteen chapters, will be referred to as R 1.

2. In 1902 Père Mandonnet, commenting on Sabatier's discovery of the Capestrano text, called attention to the mention of a fourteenth-century MS. formerly in the library of the Convent of SS. John and Paul, Venice, and described in 1755 by Berardelli in his Catalogue of that Conventual Library as having the following title:

Memoriale propositi fratrum et sororum de poenitentia in domibus propriis existentium. Inceptum anno domini MCCXXI, tale est.

It begins with the words : *Viri qui huius fraternitatis fuerint* and ends : *tanquam contumax obligetur ad culpam*. These words are identical respectively with the first words of chapter i and the last words of chapter xii of R 1.

This MS. is at present lost. Père Mandonnet and H. Boehmer have both made fruitless inquiries for it. The library of the convent was dispersed in the early part of the nineteenth century.*

3. Bernard de Bessa, writing about 1290, states that the Rule was the joint production of S. Francis himself and Pope Gregory IX:

In regulis seu vivendi formis ordinis istorum dictandis sacrae memoriae dominus papa Gregorius in minori adhuc officio constitutus, beato Francisco intima familiaritate coniunctus, devote supplebat, quod viro sancto in dictandi scientia deerat.

4. On March 30, 1228, the Bull *Detestanda* † was issued, conferring certain privileges and exemptions upon the members of the Third Order.

5. A version of the Rule, differing from R 1 but containing a large portion of the material of the first twelve chapters of R 1, is contained in Wadding's *Beati Patris Francisci Assisiatis Opera Omnia*, 1623, and in other later writers based upon Wadding. This version is generally divided into twenty chapters. It will be referred to as R 2.

6. On November 21, 1234,‡ Gregory IX issued letters to the

---

* It may be worth mention, in order to save trouble to other students, that the present editor in August, 1913, also made a search in Venice for this MS. He ascertained that there were only three public collections in Venice which were known to contain volumes from this convent, viz. the library of S. Mark, the Museo Civico which received the Cicogna Bequest, and the State Record Office in the Frari. He went through the catalogues of all three institutions and consulted the librarians, but failed to find the MS. It must have passed into private hands, if it has not perished. (See note, p. 24.)

† Sbaralea, i, p. 39.   ‡ Potthast, 9768.

Bishops placing the Tertiaries under the protection of the Bishops, and at the same time committing to them the visitation and correction of the Tertiaries.

7. A version of the Rule, substantially the same as R 2 in arrangement and contents, but nevertheless differing from it in certain respects, is incorporated in Nicholas IV's Bull *Supra Montem* of August 18, 1289. This is the version of which the text here published is a translation. It will be referred to as R 3. The best Latin text is contained in *Seraphicae Legislationis Textus Originales*, Quaracchi, 1897. This is the Rule which governed the Third Order from 1289 until 1883, when the Order was reformed by Leo XIII's Bull *Misericors*.

8. On August 8, 1290, Nicholas IV published a Bull *Unigenitus Dei Filius*,* with a view to overcoming the hostility with which R 3 was received in some quarters. The most important sentence in this Bull is as follows:—

Ordinem ipsum approbando, ordinationes nonnullas salutaris persuasionis, nostris litteris in eodem Ordine duximus observandas; inter caeteras eisdem fratribus, paterno consulentes affectu, ut huiusmodi normam vivendi sequerentur, et sequendo amplecterentur eamdem. Et cum naturalis persuadeat ratio et rationi aequitas acquiescat, ut praedicti Ordinis professores, ob ipsius Confessoris reverentiam dilectorum filiorum nostrorum Ordinis Minorum dirigantur et regulentur doctrina, qui utriusque Ordinis alumnus extitit institutor, de Ordine supradicto Fratrum Minorum visitatores et informatores assumere procurent.

Other documents of lesser importance could be mentioned, especially other Papal Bulls relating to the Tertiaries, but the documents already mentioned are those which are most important for a study of the Rule.

Something must first be said as to the date at which the Tertiaries were founded, a question which at once brings us into a region of some uncertainty. Here again it is safest to start from a fixed point, viz. a Papal document, and that fixed point is provided by the letter of Honorius III, dated December 16, 1221, to the Bishop of Rimini, which makes the first official reference to the Franciscan Tertiaries and recommends their protection: *Significatum est nobis quod Faventiae et in quibusdam*

* Potthast, 23355.

aliis civitatibus et locis vicinis quidam sunt, quibus illum Dominus inspiravit affectum ut . . . semetipsos ad poenitentiam se converterent. This letter is sufficient to show that at any rate by the date December 1221, the Order of Penitents had come into existence, and it may indicate that Faenze was the place of their origin. On the other hand, Mariano of Florence, whose authority as a sixteenth-century writer is not particularly high, claims that the first congregation of Penitents was established by S. Francis and Hugolino (Gregory IX) at Florence, in May 1221, a statement the accuracy of which is challenged by Boehmer. The traditional view has been that the Order was founded by S. Francis soon after his return from the East in 1221, in order to meet the need of the large multitude of lay folk, both men and women, who were anxious to 'do penance', but who owing to the circumstances of their lives could not become members of the First or Second Orders. Fourteenth-century tradition, as given by Bartolomeo de Tolomaeis, even specifies the names of the first members of the Third Order as Luchesio and Bonadonna, citizens of Poggibonsi. There is no evidence for the 'Luchesio' story earlier than the fourteenth century. The Bollandists have further confused the issue by identifying Luchesio with Lucius, mentioned by S. Antonino of Florence as being the first member of the Third Order.*

The authority of both Thomas of Celano and of the 'Three Companions' has been invoked for tracing the existence of the Third Order to an even earlier period, indeed to a period contemporaneous with the early preaching of S. Francis before his journey to the East; it must, however, be remembered that there is a tendency with these writers, even though they are describing events within their own lifetime, to ascribe much which was actually later to the early days of the Order, somewhat at the

---

* Curiously enough, both names are mentioned in the Latin extract from Bernardine de Bustis—contained in the Pennant MS. and printed on pp. 55-7. It will be seen that Bernardine places S. Luchesio at the beginning of his list preceded only by S. Louis and S. Ivo, and that he says of S. Lucius that he was *primus sanctus de isto tercio ordine*. This may be a clue to the way in which the whole story has originated. Lucius, who has never been canonized, but only beatified (Festival on April 15), has perhaps been confused with S. Luchesio. It is difficult to say why Bernardine describes him as he does. For it was not until long after Bernardine's time that Lucius was beatified by Innocent XII.

expense of historical accuracy and perspective. This at any rate however is certain, that the Third Order as a distinct organization must have come into existence by 1221.

It is scarcely then a coincidence that the first known version of the Rule, R 1, should contain the date 1221. Whatever view one may hold as to the Capestrano Document, there can be little doubt that it points to a Rule composed in 1221, which may or may not be wholly or partly contained in R 1 as it is now extant. Assuming that the Third Order received its first organized form not later than 1221 it would naturally be expected that the new organization would require a Rule.

The title of R 1 * is in itself ambiguous. The most simple and obvious way of understanding it is that of Père Mandonnet, who merely places a full stop after the numerals 1221. If this is done, R 1 appears to be the original 'Memorial' or Rule of 1221 with its first twelve chapters, with a later addition of 1228, viz. chapter xiii. Sabatier and Boehmer make emendations of the title by supplying words which they believe to have fallen out. Under their view the first twelve chapters are certainly in the main the Rule of 1221, but already subjected to a redaction in 1228; while chapter xiii contains material added not necessarily in 1228, but according to them probably later and at various periods. Both authorities see in chapter vi of R 1 an allusion to the Bull *Detestanda* of March 30, 1228, though the reality of that allusion seems questionable.† Père Mandonnet's argument, based upon the Venetian MS., has not been successfully answered. It is much to be hoped that the lost MS. will ultimately be found, so as to place beyond doubt the actual form of the Rule of 1221, and to show whether chapter vi contains the same phrase now understood as an allusion to *Detestanda* or not.‡

The next question which naturally arises is as to the authorship

---

* See p. 25.

† The clause in question is: *Omnes a iuramentis solemnibus abstineant nisi necessitate cogente in casibus a summo pontifice exceptis in sua indulgentia videlicet pro pace, fide, calumnia et testimonio.*

‡ More recent evidence has been brought to bear on this question by P. Lemmens, who has published in *Archiv. Franc. Hist.*, April 1913, a newly discovered version of the Rule of 1221 contained in Cod. 1159, Roy. Lib. of Königsberg. This version confirms Mandonnet's view as to the understanding of the Capestrano title and Sabatier's view as to the allusion to *Detestanda*.

of R 1, or rather of that part of R 1 which came into existence in 1221. On this point there is the greatest variety of opinion, ranging from those who have claimed it as the unaided work of S. Francis himself, to those who deny S. Francis any hand in it at all. There are probably few, if any, to-day who would assert the Rule of 1221 to be the unaided work of S. Francis. On the other hand, Boehmer in his *Analekten* combats the view that the Saint was in any sense its author, and in publishing the works of the Saint he classifies it neither as genuine nor doubtful, but as spurious. Reference has already been made to the testimony of Bernard de Bessa, who probably derived his information from S. Bonaventura (who was himself in direct touch with the disciples of S. Francis), that the Rule of 1221 was the joint work of S. Francis and Hugolino, afterwards Pope Gregory IX. We have evidence that Hugolino took some part in the composition of the Rule of the Friars Minor in 1223, and there is reason to think that he also participated in writing the Rule of the Clarisses in 1218-19. There is no good reason to doubt the testimony of Bernard de Bessa, and it is not unsafe to attribute the Form of R 1 to Hugolino and its contents to S. Francis. This is the view taken by Père Mandonnet, as well as by Jörgensen and Father Cuthbert in their recent biographies of the Saint. After all, the extant body of undoubtedly genuine writings of S. Francis is so limited as to make it somewhat unsafe to argue, as Boehmer does, that R 1 cannot be in any sense the work of S. Francis, because it is so different from his ordinary style.

The Capestrano Rule, R 1, gives then a fixed point, namely, the date 1228 as the year of the composition of part or perhaps the whole of it. Sixty-one years later another fixed point is provided by the Bull *Supra Montem*, dated August 18, 1289, and containing a new Rule, R 3. What then lies between R 1 of 1228 and R 3 of 1289?

Somewhere between these two dates lies R 2, the Rule as known to Luke Wadding, the seventeenth-century chronicler, and published by him. At first sight it might be supposed that the differences between R 2 and R 3 are so small that they are in reality the same Rule. The differences, however, though perhaps few and slight in extent, are important, and serve, taken along with other facts, as a clue to the processes lying behind the evolution of R 3. They may even at the same time throw light on the authorship of R 2.

Père Mandonnet * has worked out a theory showing how the various versions of the Rule of the Third Order reflect in their provisions the conflict which went on in the Franciscan Order between the Conventuals and those of the Strict Observance from a date even anterior to the death of the Founder. Into the precise meaning of the sundry titles given to the officers of the Order in R 1, viz. Ministers, Visitor, and the Spiritual Counsellor, later called Director, and what these terms exactly connote it is not possible to enter here, nor is it necessary, as the subject has been so fully discussed by Père Mandonnet and others. An examination of chapters i-xii of R 1, i.e. of the portion of R 1 which is mainly assignable to 1221, will show that although the Order of Penitents owed its origin to S. Francis and the movement which he founded, there is not a phrase or provision in those chapters which indicate a link between the Penitents and the Friars Minor. Neither the Visitor nor the Director need be a Friar Minor. On the contrary, the first chapters of R 1 define that the Director must be a religious, thus expressly leaving it open whether he is to be a Friar Minor or a religious of some other Order. In other words, the provisions of 1221 aim at separating the Penitents from the influence of the Friars Minor. The opposite process characterizes the provisions of chapter xiii, i.e. of 1228. Under these provisions a Friar Minor is to be placed as spiritual director to the congregation,† and the monthly gathering is to be in the 'place' of the Friars Minor. The Order of Penitents is thus deliberately brought back into a closer connexion with the Friars Minor. The alterations are so marked that they can scarcely fail to be a matter of intention. Now it will further be found that if R 2 as known to Wadding is

---

* *Opuscules de Crit. histor.* Fasc. IV, pp. 206-45.

† 4. *Item visitator et ministri huius fraternitatis petant a ministro vel custode fratrum Minorum unum fratrem Minorem de conventu, cuius fratris consilio et voluntate fratrum ista fraternitas gubernetur in omnibus et regatur.* 5. *Et quando ille frater recederet de conventu, petant alium loco eius, ita quod semper consilio fratrum Minorum regatur ista fraternitas que a beato Francisco habuit fundamentum.* 6. *Item omnes fratres conveniant in prima dominica cuiuslibet mensis ad missam in loco fratrum Minorum.*

compared with R 3, contained in the Bull *Supra Montem* of 1289, the same process is at work. Leaving aside for the time the question of the date of R 2, it will be seen that in R 2 the Visitor must be a priest of some recognized religious Order, but there is neither a direction nor even a suggestion that he should be a Franciscan; moreover the work of Visitor must not be done by any other. Now in R 3 an effort is again made, due no doubt to the influence of Nicholas IV, who had himself been a Minister General of the Franciscan Order, to restore the dominance of the Friars Minor in the counsels of the Penitents. Under chapter xx of R 3* the Visitors and Directors of the Penitents are to be Friars Minor nominated for the purpose by the 'Custodes' of the Franciscan Order; and it is defined that the Visitor must not be a layman. A smaller indication of the trend of policy is in chapter viii of R 3, where it is provided that those who labour may eat thrice a day from Easter until S. Francis's Day (October 4), instead of until Michaelmas as in R 2. To what date then, between 1228 and 1289, must the promulgation of R 2 be assigned? The date cannot be fixed with any degree of certainty, but an indication is afforded by the letters of Gregory IX, issued on November 21, 1234, by which the correction and visitation of the Tertiaries is committed to the Bishops. R 2 probably came into existence about 1234.

Thus, just as the process of separating the Penitents from the Franciscan Order in 1221 was reversed in 1228, so the same process which characterized R 2 in or about 1234 was reversed in 1289. In 1221 the influence which was dominant in the Franciscan Order was that of Elias of Cortona. In that year the Chapter had been held at which Elias had been called to the government of the Order; in that year the first outward organization of the Order of Penitents had taken place; in that year the Rule in its first form had been written. Even if Bernard de Bessa is right in his account of its authorship, that it was a joint work of S. Francis and Hugolino, it may be supposed that the dominating personality of Elias was not altogether absent in its composition. It was assuredly no part of the plan of S. Francis that that which he regarded as the one spiritual family should be split up, and that the Penitents should be

* See page 54.

segregated from the Friars Minor. The policy represented by the Rule of 1221 was the policy of Elias and also of Hugolino. From 1226-32 Elias was under a cloud; his policy no longer guided the Order; the Friars of the Strict Observance had gained the upper hand. But about 1232 Elias returned to power, and held the position of Minister General until his deposition in 1239. By 1234 Hugolino had been raised to the Pontificate as Gregory IX, and Elias was still in his counsels and was trusted by him. It is somewhat unlikely that the Rule of 1234 would be drafted by the Pope himself. It is quite possible that in R 2 the handiwork of Elias himself may be seen. There is no documentary evidence in support of this theory, nor is there any to refute it. Given the facts that the Rule, known to Wadding, came into existence about 1234, and that it reflects faithfully the known policy of Elias, there is scarcely any person to whom the responsibility for the changes of 1234 and the composition of R 2 can be with more probability assigned than Elias of Cortona.

While the general accuracy of this explanation of the history of the evolution of the Rules of the Third Order may be admitted, too much weight must not be attached to it, especially so far as the early form of R 1 is concerned. There may be another reason why R 1 contains no reference to the Friars Minor, and why it is not until 1228 that the visitation of the Tertiaries is committed to them. The Tertiaries in the nature of things, whether originally as individuals or later as congregations, were people with fixed abodes. The Friars Minor in the early years of the Order were without any such abodes. Even if in some districts it would have been possible to rely on their services as Visitors or Directors of the Tertiaries, it could not until a later period have been uniformly possible. This consideration, which affects equally the visitation of the Clarisses, has been effectively pointed out by Père Livarius Oliger in his *De Originę Regularum Ordinis S. Clarae.**

In the present somewhat incomplete state of knowledge regarding the early beginnings of the Franciscan Order and of the forces at work in the composition of the Rules, this fact is one for which room must be left in theories as to the Rules.

* *Archiv. Franc. Histor.* Tom. v. Fasc. II, p. 202.

The English Version of the Rule.

Having thus considered briefly the history and constitution of the Third Order of S. Francis or *Ordo de Poenitentia*, it remains to consider the special characteristics of the English version of the Rule here published.

It will first be observed that this version begins with a list of chapter headings or table of contents which is not found in the published Latin originals. It is an addition made probably for the convenience of the English Tertiaries for whom this copy of the Rule was written. The chapter headings thus given correspond exactly to the rubricated headings which introduce each chapter in the text. For the most part the English headings are close translations of the traditional chapter headings of the Latin Rule. It will, however, at once be noticed that, whereas the Latin Rule as generally found is divided into twenty chapters, the present version has been divided into twenty-four chapters. Before considering the reasons for this, it will be well to set out the divisions comparing the English text with the Latin text as published by the Quaracchi Fathers.*

Pennant MS.	*Quaracchi Text.*
Chap. I. Of the catholik faith, &c.	Preamble not treated as a separate chapter.
Chap. II.	Chap. I and Chap. II, to 'proximis reconciliare procuret'.
Chap. III.	Chap. II. From 'quibus omnibus ad effectum productis' to 'solicita consideratione discussis'.
Chap. IV.	Chap. II. From 'Ordinamus praeterea' to end.
Chap. V.	Chap. III.
Chap. VI.	Chap. IV.
Chap. VII.	Chap. V down to 'tribus vicibus Pater Noster'.

* *Seraphicae Legislationis Textus Originales*, 1897, pp. 77-96.

Pennant MS.	Quaracchi Text.
Chap. VIII.	Chap. V. From 'Qualibet vero' to 'noscitur institutum'.
Chap. IX.	Chap. VI.
Chap. X.	Chap. VII.
Chap. XI.	Chap. VIII.
Chap. XII.	Chap. IX.
Chap. XIII.	Chaps X and XI.
Chap. XIV.	Chap. XII.
Chap. XV.	Chap. XIII to 'inibi audituri'.
Chap. XVI.	Chap. XIII. From 'unusquisque autem' to 'et inducat'.
Chap. XVII.	Chap. XIII. From 'Studeat quilibet' to end.
Chap. XVIII.	Chap. XIV.
Chap. XIX.	Chap. XV.
Chap. XX.	Chap. XVI.
Chap. XXI.	Chap. XVII.
Chap. XXII.	Chap. XVIII.
Chap. XXIII.	Chap. XIX.
Chap. XXIV.	Chap. XX.

It is difficult to suppose that it is mere chance which has caused the writer of the Pennant text to divide his Rule into twenty-four chapters instead of twenty. The explanation is possibly much the same as that which Père Mandonnet * suggests in support of his theory that the so-called Capestrano Rule consisted of an original Rule of 1221 divided into twelve chapters, to which were added, in 1228, later additions forming a thirteenth chapter.† He attributes it to the important place occupied by the numeral 12 in Franciscan thought. He claims that the Rule of the Friars Minor of 1223 and that of the Clarisses were both divided into 12

* *L'Ordo de Poenitentia.* Opuscules de Crit. histor. Fasc. IV, pp. 156-7.
† This theory of Mandonnet is, however, much injured by Lemmens's discovery that the text in the Königsberg MS. is divided into eight chapters (see note, p. 29).

chapters; that as a parallel to the apostolic band of 12, S. Francis had 12 chief companions: that the Apostles' Creed consists of 12 articles. 'Ce que le Symbole était pour l'Église primitive, les règles Franciscaines devaient l'être pour chacune des fractions de l'ordre.'

It is true that Père Mandonnet's theory on this point has been severely criticized by Père Livarius Oliger, O.F.M., who in his two articles 'De Origine Regularum Ordinis S. Clarae,'* points out that, if we go back to the original Papal Bulls which are preserved, neither headings nor divisions of chapters appear, and that such divisions are arbitrary. It remains a significant fact that the 'arbitrary' division of the Rules of the First and Second Order, from whatever epoch the divisions date, do favour the numeral 12. And referring to the Pennant version of the Rule of the Third Order, it seems an inevitable conclusion that either the translator was translating from a Rule divided into twenty chapters and that he deliberately re-arranged his material so as to form twenty-four: or that having before him a Rule without any chapter divisions, he still divided his material into twenty-four. This latter possibility is very remote, for it will be seen that in the large majority of cases he translates the traditional chapter headings.

Another peculiarity of the English version will be found in chapter xix; in order to make this clear it is necessary to set out the English and Latin side by side:

| Eche of theme also muste devoutly take upon theme all other occupacions and offices enioyned theme that this reule requireth and treuly execute them. Also every officer shalbe but for a tyme *and none for terme of lyffe*. | Ministeria quoque ac alia officia, quae praesentis formulae series exprimit, imposita sibi quisque devote suscipiat, curetque fideliter exercere. Officium autem cuiuslibet certi temporis spatio limitetur. *Nullus Minister instituatur ad vitam et eius ministerium certum terminum comprehendat.* |

The words in italics show how the English writer has slightly altered his material and curtailed his translation. The Latin text expressly states that no Minister is to hold office for life: the

* *Archiv. Franc. Histor.* Tom. v. Fasc. II and III. An. 1912, p. 431.

English text says 'none for terme of lyffe' but does not specify the Ministers. This may be a somewhat slender foundation, but it does suggest that in the place or places where this English version was current, it was not convenient to specify too exactly the conditions of tenure of the Ministers. It will be seen that the repeated injunction *eius ministerium certum terminum comprehendat* is left untranslated.

In chapter v the text as given on page 49 shows how a later hand has corrected the original version and brought it into line with the Latin original. It would appear that the first hand resorted to abbreviation, because he could not find the English equivalents of the Latin names of certain vestments. It will be noticed that whereas the English prescribes for the Sisters 'a wyde palumdelum of lynnen clothe', the Latin original gives 'paludellum amplum *de cannabo*, sive lino,' or as the Pont. Reg. gives, *de canape*.

A slight error in the closing words of the Bull is sufficient to show that the Pennant MS. is almost certainly a copy of a translation made probably by a scribe not very familiar with Latin, and that it is not the work of the actual translator. The word *Kalender* instead of *Kalendes* suggests that the scribe was unfamiliar with the Latin system of chronology.

The Quaracchi Fathers of the 'Collegium Sanctae Bonaventurae' have shown in their edition of the Rule of the Third Order in the *Seraphicae Legislationis Textus Originales*,* that there are certain variants as between the Latin text generally published (e.g. in Sbaralea's Bullarium) and the more authoritative text contained in the Pontifical Register of the Vatican. An examination of the Pennant MS. will show that it is a translation of a text which in the main agrees with the more accurate text of the Pontifical Register; in one passage, however, it departs from the Pontifical Register reading in favour of the traditional reading; in another the original text agrees with the Register, while the later correction does not. The points of agreement and disagreement are as follows:

Preamble. 'The way to come to God.' Pont. Reg. *viam accedendi*. Traditional text, *viam ascendendi*.

* Quaracchi, 1897, pp. 9 and 77-96.

Chap. III (Penn). 'Of his instaunce.' Pont. Reg. *instantia.*
Trad. text, *instantis.*

Chap. III (Penn). 'The whiche all thinges so done.' Pont.
Reg. *Quibus omnibus ad effectum perductis.* Trad. text, *productis.*

Chap. V (Penn). 'A guarnellum ... made withoute any
wrynkylle.' Pont. Reg. *guarnellum ... consutum.* Trad. text,
garnellum ... consuetum.

Chap. XVIII (Penn). 'Over this euery brother,' &c. Pont. Reg.
Et praeter haec. Trad. text, *et post haec.*

Finale. 'And if eny presume to attempte.' Pont. Reg. *ausu
temerario.* Trad. text, *usu temerario.*

On the other hand:

Preamble. 'That promitteth the great rewardes.' Trad. text,
praemia grandia. But Pont. Reg. *praemia gaudiaque.*

Chap. V (Penn). 'Vesture clasped close and not opyn.' Pont. Reg.
non patulas. Trad. text, *vel patulas.* But the correction in later
hand has 'kut or hole *but* opyn', thus departing from Pont. Reg.

Other variants exist as between the two Latin texts, but they
are too slight to affect the English translation. But the examination of the variants given above is sufficient to show that the
Pennant translator has had direct or indirect access to the text
of the Pontifical Register, which in the matter of every variant is
superior to the traditional text. It would appear further that
the second scribe who added the correction in chapter v used the
traditional text in spite of the words 'but opyn' giving such bad
sense and that he probably did not fully understand his original,
as he left the words *guarnellum, placentinum,* and *palumdelum*
untranslated. The variant *grandia* (great rewards) in the Preamble
is difficult to explain. Somehow this inferior reading must have
crept into the Latin text which the Pennant translator was
using.

The Pennant Manuscript.

The version of the Rule of the Third Order of S. Francis which
is here published, is contained in a manuscript which has recently
come into the possession of the editor. The manuscript is on
thick vellum and measures 193 mm. × 130 mm. It consists of
19 leaves. The first leaf contains an illuminated picture of the

Stigmatization of S. Francis, measuring 130 mm. × 90 mm. Leaves 2–14 inclusive contain the English version of the Rule of the Third Order; the writing is in black, with the chapter headings and some proper names in red. The index of the several chapters occupies leaves 2 and 3. This portion of the manuscript is written in a neat and legible English hand of the latter half of the fifteenth century; there are generally 19 lines to the page.

Leaves 15 and 16 contain a Latin fragment beginning *De tercio eciam ordine Beatus Franciscus produxit multos flores*. This fragment is an extract from the twenty-seventh sermon of Bernardine de Bustis' *Rosarium Sermonum predicabilium*,* Part II. It is written in a different and smaller hand from that of leaves 2–14, and is certainly a later addition; the hand appears to be Italian. This portion of the manuscript contains 22 lines to the page, and the capital initials are written alternately in blue and red with great regularity. There is a finely illuminated initial D with elaborate scroll-work at the beginning of the Latin fragment. The Latin text consists of a list of the more important members of the Third Order, both men and women, including all those who at the time when Bernardine wrote, i.e. in the last quarter of the fifteenth century, had been canonized or beatified.

Leaves 17, 18, 19 contain illuminated pictures of Christ being taken prisoner in Gethsemane and of Christ before Pilate. Facing these are the twelve *Paternosters* and *Glorias* for Matins, and the seven *Paternosters*, the *Glorias*, the *Credo*, and the *Miserere* for Compline in accordance with the requirements of chapter xi of the Rule. The pages containing the Offices for the intervening hours have unfortunately been cut out, doubtless for the sake of the illuminations.

The history of the manuscript so far as it can be traced is as follows. It was one of the manuscripts acquired by the well-known antiquary and bibliophile, Thomas Pennant (1726–98), for his collection at Downing, Flintshire. The library of Thomas Pennant, including the Downing property, passed to Louisa Pennant, his great-grand-daughter, who was the first wife of the late Lord Denbigh. She died without issue some years afterwards, and left the property to her husband, from whom it passed to the present Lord Denbigh, his son by a second marriage. The

---

* Printed at Venice in 1498 by Georgius de Arrivabenis.

chief portion of the Downing Collection, including the present manuscript, was sold by auction at Messrs. Sotheby's in March, 1913, and was ultimately purchased by the editor. It is now at University College Hall, Ealing. There is no means of ascertaining from what source Thomas Pennant acquired it, probably in the middle of the eighteenth century. Unfortunately, the manuscript, which was unbound, gives no clue to show in what place in England it was written or for whom; nor is it profitable to conjecture whether it was written for some individual Tertiary as a private book of devotion or for a Community. This manuscript version in the English language is certainly rare, possibly unique. There appears to be no English manuscript of the Rule of the Third Order either in the British Museum or in the Bodleian Library, nor has the editor heard of another similar manuscript, though others perhaps exist.

BIBLIOGRAPHY

Adderley, J. G., and *Marson, C. L.* Third Orders. London, 1902.
Boehmer, H. Analekten zur Geschichte des Franciscus von Assisi. Pp. xxxi-xxxv. Tübingen, 1904.
Cuthbert, Father, O.S.F.C. Life of Saint Francis of Assisi. Book iii, chap. vi. & Appendix iii. London, 1912.
Goetz, W. Die Regel des Tertiarierordens. Zeit. für Kirchengeschichte, vol. xxiii, 1902.
Heimbucher, Max. Die Orden und Kongregationen der katholischen Kirche. Vol. 2, pp. 489–527. Paderborn, 1902. (This work contains on page 489 a bibliography of older works on the Third Order.)
Jörgensen, J. Saint Francis of Assisi: A Biography. Chapter x. London, 1912.
Mandonnet, Rev. Pierre. Les origines de l'Ordo de Pœnitentia. Compte rendu du quatrième Congrès scientifique international des Catholiques. Freiburg, 1898.
Mandonnet, Rev. Pierre. Les Règles et le Gouvernement de l'Ordo de Pœnitentia au XIIIe siècle. Opuscules de Critique historique. Paris, 1902.
Müller, Dr. Karl. Die Anfänge des Minoritenordens und der Bussbruderschaften. Freiburg, 1885.
Sabatier, Paul. Regula antiqua fratrum et sororum de Pœnitentia. Opuscules de Critique historique. Paris, 1901.
Sabatier, Paul. Nouveaux travaux sur les documents Franciscains. Opuscules de Critique historique. Paris, 1903.
Seraphicae Legislationis Textus Originales. Quaracchi, 1897.
Works of St. Francis of Assisi. Translated by a Religious of the Order. London (R. Washbourne), 1890.

THE THIRDE ORDER OF
SEYNT FRANCEYS

FOR THE BRETHREN AND SUSTERS OF
THE ORDER OF PENITENTIS

[*Note.*—Contractions universally recognized are not indicated in the text. For instance, the scribe signified *m* or *n* sometimes by writing it in full, sometimes by putting a stroke over a preceding vowel. Which of these two methods he preferred to use in any particular word is of no more interest than which of two possible forms of the letter *r* or *s* he may have preferred.

Italics are therefore reserved in order to indicate that the editor is departing from the MS. Where a letter is changed, that letter is put in italics and the MS. reading given in a footnote. Where a letter or a word is supplied, it is placed in italics between square brackets. This rule naturally applies to the English only. All Latin is in italics. The more common contractions are expanded without comment; more elaborate expansions forced upon the editor by the necessity of making his Latin intelligible are placed between square brackets.

This Note refers only to the Text of the Rule of the 'Thirde Order of Seynt Franceys' and to that of the Rule of 'Sustris Menouresses enclosid'.]

Here beginnyth the Chapituris of the iii^{de} order of [Fol. 2^r] Seynt franceys for the Brethren and Susters of the order of Penitentis.¹

Of the catholike feyth of the Brethren and Susters of this reule. Ca^m. j.

Of the comyng of the brethren and susters to this reule. Capi̇m. ij.

Of the receyuyng to profession of þe brethren and susters of this reule.   Ca^m. iij.

How it shall not be leafull to the brethren and susters after they be come in to go oute of this reule.   Capi̇m. iiij.

Of the vesture or clothing of the brethren and susters of this rule. Ca^m. v.

How it is forboden going to eny wondringis, gasingis or to eny dishonest festis to the brethren & susters of this reule. Capi̇m. vj.

Of the abstinence frome Fleshe eting comaundid to the brethren [Fol. 2^v] and susters of this reule.   Capi̇m. vij.

Of the fasting of the brethren and susters of this reule. Capi̇m. viij.

Of confession and comynion of the brethren and susters of this reule.   Cap.^m. ix.

How it is forboden eny wepyn to be borne by the brethren of this reule.   Capi̇tulum x.

Of prayer of the bretherne and susters of this reule.   Capitı̇m. xj.

Of the testamentis of the brethren and susters of this reule. Capi^m. xij.

Of pece keping of the brethren and susters of this reule. Capi^m. xiij.

How swering is forboden to the brethren and susters of þis reule. Ca^m. xiiij.

Of hering of masse of the brethren and susters of þis reule. Ca^m. xv.

Of almus doing of þe brethren and susters of this reule. Cap^m. xvj. [Fol. 3^r]

¹ The notes to which this and subsequent numbers relate will be found on pp. 58, 59.

Of scilens keping in the Chirche of the brethren and susters of þis reule.   Cap^m. xvij.

Of the brethren & susters that be seke or dye after they bo enterid into this reule.   Ca^m. xviij.

5 Of office bering of the brethren of this reule.   Capitulum xix.

How the visitour shall visit þe brethren and susters of this reule. Capi^m. xx.

Of the exchewing of striues and debatis emonge the brethren and susters of this reule.   Cap^m. xxj.

10 Of the dispensacion of Fastingis with the brethren and susters of this reule.   Capitulum xxij.

Of suche as be incorrigible brethren and susters of this reule. Capi^m. xxiij.

How that this reule and order byndith not vnder payne of deadely
[Fol. 3^v]   synne eny of the bretherne and susters of this reule.   Capitulum xxiiij.

In the name of god here beginnith the reule of [Fol. 4ʳ] the liuing of the brethrene and susters of the order of penitentis.

Of the catholik feith of the bretherne and susters of this reule. Caplm. j.

NICHOLAS [2] Busshoppe seruaunt of the seruauntes of god. To oure welbelouid sonnes the bretherne and to oure welbelouid doughters in criste the susters of the order of the brethren of penaunce as well to them that be present as to suche as shal be in tyme to come, Gretyng and the apostolik blessing. IT IS KNOWEN þat the stedfast grounde and foundement of cristen religion is sett vppon the hill of the vniuersall feithe the whiche þe clene | deuocion of cristes discipuls brennyng with the fyre of [Fol. 4ᵛ] charite taught with the worde of besy predicacion the peple of Jentils that walked in derkeness. The which also the churche of Rome holdith & kepith, whose foundement and grounde neuer shalbe cast doune with troubles nor brosid with no flodes of tempestes, for this is the right and trew feith, withoute whose company no man is accepted nor may haue grace in the sight of god. IT IS he þat geuith the way to saluacion and þat promittith the great rewardes of euerlasting felicite. THERFOR the glorius confessor of criste Saint Frannceys the founder of this order, shewing in worde and dede þe way to come to god taught his children in the clennes of the saide feithe & wolde that they shulde be professed therin & stedfastly kepe it and fulfill it [Fol. 5ʳ] in deade, so | that they walking heilfully by the same wey might deserue to be made possessioners of euerlasting blisse after the disseace of this present lyfe.

Of the comyng of the brethren and susters to this reule. Capitulum ij.

WE* THERFOR willing to depart oure fauor to the seid order and for the encrease of the same haue stabilyshte and ordeyned that all tho that shalbe receyued to the seid order before ther

* MS. HE corrected in margin.

admission or rescey[u]ing* shalbe examened diligently of their
feith and obedience toward the forsaide chirche of rome. And
yf they beleue treuly and stedfastly, then they may be resceyuid
suerly to the same order. Neuerthelesse it is to be ware
diligently that none heretike or suspect of heresy[3] or noysed
theruppon be admittyd in eny wyse to þe obseruaunce | of this lyfe
And yf eny suche were founde that he be comytted anon to the
Inquisitoures of heresies to be ponyshid by theme. Also when
eny shalbe admitted to enter into this fraternite, the mynisters
that bene deputed to receyue them shall enquire diligently of his
office astate and condicion, declaring to them the charges of this
fraternite, and specially that tha must restore all that thay haue
of oder mennes goodes, and after þat, if it pleasith þam, they
shalbe clothed after the forme of the reule. And then if thaye
haue ony goodes of other mennes, they must restore it in monye
or after the cawcion of the pleggis.[4] And be reconsiled neuerthelesse to their neyghbor.

Of the resceyuing to profession of the brethern and susters of þis
reule. Ca^m. iij.

The ‡ whiche all thinges so done after the space of oone yere w^t
the councell and aduyse of sume of the discrete bretherne, if they
thinke that he be worthy he shalbe receyued in this maner, That
is for to sey that he shall promitte to kepe all the commaundementis of god and make satisfaccion of all trespases that he shall
do ayenst this maner liuing to the will of the visitour whan he
shalbe required by hym, the whiche promes so made by hym
shalbe wrytte by a notary in an Instrument. And that none be
receyued otherwise by the seid ministers w^{t}oute hem thought[5] to
be done by the consideracion of the persons condicion and of his
instaunce and Desyre.

How it shall not be leafull to þe brethern and susters after they
be come in to go | owte of this reule. Capīm. iiij.

Ouer this we ordeyne and stablisshe that none aftyr that he is
come to this fraternite may retorne in to the worlde but he may
haue neuertheles fre going in to eny other approued religion.[6]
And as for women that haue husbondes they shall not come in to
the seide fraternite but by the concent & licence of theme.

* MS. 'resceying'.   † 'haue' is added in later hand.
‡ MS. Ebe corrected in margin to The.

Of the vesture & clothing of the Bretherne and Susters of þis reule. Capitulum v.

FURTHERMORE the bretherne of this fraternite shalbe comynly clothed with meke clothes in price and coloure not all whyte or all blacke wᵗoute it be dispensid with some by the visitours of the councell of the mynysters of the price of the clothe⁷ for a tyme & for a lawfull & an open | cause. The forseid bretherne also shall haue * vesture clasped close and not opyn before as honesti requirith and closed slevis. The susters also shall haue vesture made wᵗ soche meke clothe. AND as for mekenes of the clothes and furres of the susters it may be dispensed after the condicion of iche of theme and after the custome of the countrey. They shall not vse boundes and gyrdilles of sylke. Also the bretherne as well as the susters shall haue no furres but of lame skynnes and purses of lether and gerdillis wᵗoute eny silke & none other, All other vayne araye of the worlde layde aparte after the holsome councell of the prince of the apostels. [Fol. 7ʳ]

How it is forboden goyng to eny wondryngis, gasingis or to eny dishonest festis to the bretherne and susters of this reule. Capitulum vj.

THEY SCHALL not go in no wise to no dishonest festis dyners or sopers, nor to no gasingis or wonndring places nor to lordes courtes or daunces. They shall not also geue enything to Joglers or mynstrellis for loue of ther vaniteis and they shall forbid to their seruauntes that they gyue theim no thing. [Fol. 7ᵛ]

Of the abstinence frome fleshe eting comaundid to the brethern and susters of this reule. Capiᵐ. vij.

ECHE OF THEIM shall absteyne frome fleshe eting the Moundey, Wednisday, Friday & Saterday withoute that they must do otherwise by cause of sekenes or febilnes of body. And as to theme that be lett bloode, they may ete fleshe iij Dayes. And they þat travell by the way may also ete fleshe all that while. ALSO

---

* A later hand has deleted four lines from 'vesture . . . clothe' and has added in the lower margin : 'mantelles and pylches wᵗowte Scalatura kut or hole but opyn as honesty reqwireth and closyd sleves. The susters also shall haue mantelle and curtelle mayd wᵗ suche meke cloth or at the leste they shall haue wᵗ the mantelle a guarnellum or else a placentinum of whyte or els of blak or a wyde palumdelum of lynnen clothe made wᵗoute any wrynkylle.'

E

The Thirde Order of Seynt Frunceys

[Fol. 8ʳ] euery one of theim | may ete fleshe in principall festis whan other cristen men of olde custome do ete fleshe, and in other dayes þat be not fastyng thay may ete eggis and chese but whan they come in ony howse of religion they may ete soche as is sett before theme. Also they must holde theme content wᵗ ij meles a day dyner and soper except tho that bene seke or traveling by the way. They that bene hoole must ete & drinke temperatly, for asmoche as the gospel seithe 'Loke that your hartis be no greuid with gloteney and drounkenesse'. Euermore befor dyner and before soper they shall saye a PATER NOSTER, and aftyr euery mele a nother PATER NOSTER, wᵗ DEO GRACIAS, and if tha fayle so to doo they shall say PATER NOSTER thries þerfor.

Of the fasting of the bretherne & susters of this reule. Capitulum viij.

[Fol. 8ᵛ] THEY SCHALL fast euery Friday of the yere withoute eny sekenes or other laufull cause lett theme or without cristemasse day fall vpon the friday. FROME alhalowtide vnto ester day thei shall fast wednisday and friday and they must kepe neuerthelesse all oþer fasting dayes that bene ordeynde by the churche and þat be commaundid by the ordinaryes for a comyn cause. In seint martin lente⁸ vnto Cristemas day and frome the sonday of Quinquagesime tyll ester day they muste faste euery day excepte sondayes withoute sekenes or eny other cause lett theme. The susters that bene with childe vnto the day of þer purificacion if they will shall do no thynge of bodeley occupacion except prayers. THEI that labore for cause of ther werines frome estyr tyll [Fol. 9ʳ] seint FRAUNCEYS⁹ may | ete laufully thries in the day whan they laubor. And when they shall worke for other men they shall ete such as is sett before them * euery day excepte fridaies or other fasting dayes ordeyned generally by the churche.

Of confession and comiuion of the brederne & susters of this reule. Capiᵐ. ix.

ALSO EUERY brother and suster iij tymes in the yere, that is Cristemasse, Ester, and Whitsontide, must be shreven and houseled¹⁰ deuoutly and be reconsiled with ther neyghbours restoring also other mennys goodes.

* 'euery day' added in a later hand.

londe . or ellis by the space of ye ministers.
Of prayer of the brethern & sisters
of the 6 reule. Capitulum . xj .

he of theme muste say every
day ther service. that is mateyns.
Prime and overs. Evynsong & Complyn .
and thei that be clarkes that can ye Saul
ter . shall say at prime . Deus i nōie
tuo . and Beati immaculati . vnto .
legem pone . whith other psalmys (wt
Gloria patri . as clerkes done . And when
thei go not to the churche they shall sey
for matens the psalmis that the clerkis
or the Cathedrall churche saithe . or ellis
as other onlerned men done . for ma
tens . vij . Pater noster . and for every
owre . vij . Pater noster . wt Aue Maria .
So that at prime . and at Complene .
they that can it shall sey oon . Crede .
and . Miserere mei deus . and if they

How it is forboden eny wepyn to be borne [11] by the bretherne
of this reule. Cap^m. x.

THE BRETHERNE shall bere with theme no wepyn withoute it
be for the defence of the churche of Rome or for the cristen faith
or for ther owne | londe or ellis by the lycens of þe ministers.   [Fol. 9ᵛ]

Of prayer of the bretherne & susters of thes reule. Capitulum xj.

ECHE OF THEME muste say euery day ther service, that is
Matyns, Prime and owers, Evynsong & Complyn [12], and thei that
be clarkes that can þe Saulter shall say at prime *DEUS, IN
NOMINE TUO* [13] and *BEATI INMACULATI* [14] vnto *LEGEM PONE* [15] whith 10
other psalmys w^t *Gloria patri*, as clerkes done. And when thei
go not to the churche they shall sey for matens the psalmis that
the clerkis or the Cathedrall churche saithe, or ellis as other
onlerned men done, For matens xij *PATER NOSTER*, and for euery
owre vij *PATER NOSTER* w^t *GLORIA PATRI*. So that at prime and 15
at Complene they that can it shall sey oon *CREDE* [16] and *MISERERE
MEI DEUS* [17], and if they | say not in dewe tymes, they muste sey [Fol. 10ʳ]
iij *PATER NOSTER*. They that be seke be not bounden to sey the
said owers w^towten they will. IN SAINT Martyn lent & also
in the great lent [18] they shall go to matens to the parishe chirche 20
wher they dwell withoute they haue a laufull excuse.

Of the Testamentes of the bretherne and Susters of this reule.
Cap^m. xij.

ALSO ICHE of them that may by the lawe muste make his
Testament and dispose his goodis anon w^tin iij monethis after 25
that they be comyn in so that none of them discese withoute
testament.

Of pece keping of the bretherne and susters of this reule.
Capitulu. xiij.

AND AS FOR peace making betwene the bretherne & susters 30
or betwixit strangers it shalbe as the | mynisters woll have it with [Fol. 10ᵛ]
the councell of the diosesan if nede be to be hade in this party.
And if the bretherne or susters wer vexed by the iuges or
gouerners of the places wherin they dwell ayenst the lawe or ther
priuileges, the mynysters of ther places must goo to the Busshopis 35
and ordinaries and must Do after þer counsell and ordinaunce.

How swering is forboden to the brethern and susters of this reule. Capi^m. xiiij.

THEY MUSTE also absteyne fro Solempne othes [19] withoute nede require it and in causes admitted by the pope, that is for the peace
5 for the faithe and for a maner of a nothe þat is callyd *De calumpnia*, for witnesse being and for contractis of byeng & selling & of Donacion wher it shall be sene expedient, and in
[Fol. 11^r] ther comen speche they | muste exchew as *moche as tha may othes and † swering. And he that eny day onwarly swerith by
10 lightnes of tounge, as it fortuneth often tymes in moche Jangeling, he must sey at euyn whan he remembrithe hym selfe what he hath done iij PATER NOSTER for soche ondescrete othes. ALSO iche of theim muste haue goode mynde to teche his seruauntes and to stere theim to goddes seruice.

15 Of hering of masse of the bretherne & susters of þis reule. Capi^m. xv.

EUERY BROTHER and suster þat hathe ther helthe, of what countre or place that so euer they be, yf they may goodly, must here masse euery day [20] and euery moneth they must appere to
20 þat chirche or place wher the mynisters shall assigne theim ther to here solempne masses.

[Fol. 11^v] Of almus doing of the bretherne and | susters of this reule. Capitulu. xvj.

ECHE OF THEME also muste geve a peny of customably money
25 to the storer,[21] the whiche shall receyve it and departe it congruently by the councel of the ministers betwixte the poore bretherne and susters and specially amonge tho that be seke and amonge suche that haue not wherwith to be buryed and aftyr that amonge the poore men.

30 FORTHERMORE they shall offer of the same money to the churche aboue saide. And then, if it may be, they shall gett theme a Religious man competently lettered, the whiche shall stere theme and enduce them besily to penance and to the fulfilling of the dedis of mercy.

* 'moche as' added in later hand. † 'and' added in later hand.

The Thirde Order of Seynt Franceys

Of * silence keping in the chi[r]che of the brethern & susters of this reule. Ca^m. xvij.

ECHE OF THEME muste kepe his silence whan the masse is † in doing, and whan the worde of gode is saide, tha must take hede to prayer and to the office withoute he be letted for cause of the comen profet of the fraternite.

Of the brethern & susters þat be seke or dye aftyr they be enterd in to þis reule. Ca^m. xviij.

AND WHEN eny of the brethern shalbe seke, the ministers must visit theim or sum other in ther place if they haue knowlege therof ones in the weke stering theim besily to penaunce in the best maner that they shall thinke expedient for theim, geffyng theim also that is necessary to theim of the comen goodes; and if eny of them disseace, | it must be notyfied to all the brethern & susters of the place wher he is deade, the whiche must be present to the deade man exequies and not Departe till the masse be done and the body be buried. And this also must be obserued to the Susters that be seke and þat disseasen. Ouer this euery brother & suster w^tin viij dayes of the obite of hym þat is disseased shall say for his soule, that is for to sey, preistis shall sey one masse for hym, and they that can þe psalter shall sey l. psalmus and they þat be vnletterd shall say l. PATER NOSTER and at the ende of iche they shall sey REQUIEM ETERNAM, and besyde all this they shall ‡ cause to be sayd euery yere iij masses for the welthe [22] of the bretherne and susters quike and deade, | and they that can þe psalter they shall say it ones and other shall sey an hunderd PATER NOSTER with REQUIEM ETERNAM & cetera at the ende of iche.

Of office bering of the bretherne of this reule. Cap^m. xix.

ECHE OF THEME also muste deuoutly take vpon theme all other occupacions & offices enioyned theme that this reule requireth and treuly execute them. Also euery officer shalbe but for a tyme and none for terme of lyffe.

* MS. reads 'licence'.
† MS. adds 'be' which is deleted and then apparently restored.
‡ MS. 'say' deleted.

How the visitoure shall visit the bretherne & susters of þis
reule. Cap^m. xx.

Also the ministers and bretherne & susters of euery Cyte and [Fol. 13ᵛ] place must gader theme in some Religiouse place or in | a chirche whan ther is no religiouse place and ther they muste haue a preist of sum religion approued, the whiche shall enioyne thame pennaunce for ther trespaces. So that none other may execute this office of visitacion vpon theme. And forasmuche that this maner of lyffing was ordeyned and stablisshed by Seynt Fraunces, we geue councell that the forseide visitores and techars be taken of the Frere menores suche as the Custodis or Wardenis of the saide order whan they be required shall assigne. And we woll in no wise that suche congregacion bene visit by laye men. And this visitacion shalbe doon ones in the yere withoute it be nedfull to be [Fol. 14ʳ] done ofter, and if eny of theme | bene rebellis and will not be corrected, aftyr thryes warnyng they shalbe put oute of the congregacion by the counsell of Discrete men.

Of the exchewing of Stryves and debatis emonge the bretherne and susters of this reule. Cap^m. xxj.

Also the br. thern & susters in all that tha may must exchewe stryves and Debates emonge theme, and if eny hap, they must besili amend it or ellis they must annswer in the lawe before hym that hathe Jurisdiction.

Of the dispensacion of fastingis withe þe bretherne and susters of this reule. Cap^m. xxij.

Also the ordinaries and visitor may despence with all the [Fol. 14ᵛ] bretherne and susters in ther | abstinences, Fastingis & other obseruaunces, whan nede causes resonabill shall require it.

Of suche as be incorrigible brethern and susters of this reule. Cap^m. xxiij.

The mynisters also shall denounce to the visitoure the opyn fautis of the bretherne & susters and he shall punyshe theme. And yf eny of theme be incorrigible[23] aftyr thryes warnyng, the ministers muste denounce theme by the councell of sum of the discrete bretherne to the visitour, the whiche shall putt hym oute of the feliship and this muste be aftyrwarde publisshid in the con[*gre*]gacion.

vere ordine pontificacion. Deo
gracias. Beatus franciscus.

De tercio et alio ordine.
Beatus franciscus produxit
multos flores. s. scm Lhi
domicu regem francie & Ze
arum comite ariam: qui cum beata delphina
vxore sua in matrimonio nitauit perpetuā virgi
nitate. Ite scm Inonem viris vtriusq̃ doc
tore pspicuū q̃ et confessore de britania minori
qui fuit magnie deuocōnis et contemplacō
nis atq̃ miraculis claruit. ac semel cū missa
celebraret in eleuacōne sacramenti. visus est
globus ignē super caput ei. Ite bm̃ luceē sem
siue lucencū de podio bonisi cui caput ego i ma
nibus habui. et est in loco nro qui est in tuscia si
monte nupiale vbi est caū corpus ei. Et monas
terium nrm appellat scī lucensis siue lucensi. Et
produxit scm luciū cōfessore qui fuit pmus scīs
de isto tercio ordine. Et scm Ncholuciū de senis
ac bm̃ Jacobū de laude sacerdote et miraclis clar.
Et beatū petrum romanū qui sub soldano sunt

How that þis reule & order byndithe not vnder payne of dedly
synne eny of þe brethern & susters of | this reule. [Fol. 15ʳ]
Capitulum xxiiij.

NEUERTHELESSE we woll not that tochyng the premisses eny
of the bretherne or susters of þe order fall in eny deadely synne 5
for soche thynges in the whiche they be not bounden by the
commaundementis of god or by the statutes of the churche but
that they resceyue mekely & affectually fulfylle soche pennaunces
as is put vpon theme for ther offencis.

Therfor be it not leafull to no maner of man to Interrupte 10
or come ayenste this oure present statute and ordinaunce.

And if eny presume to attempte ther ayenste, let hym wytt
þat he fallith in to the indignacion of almyghty god & of hys
apostles Seynt Petir and seynt Powle.

Gouen at Reate [24] the xv Kalendes *[25] of Septembre þe secunde 15
yere of oure pontificacion [26]. *Deo gracias.* [Fol. 15ᵛ]

Beatus Franciscus

DE TERCIO ECIAM ORDINE

Beatus Franciscus produxit multos flores, scilicet sanctum Ludo-
uicum regem francie, Elzearium comitem ariani, qui cum beata 20
delphina vxore sua in matrimonio iurauit † perpetuam virginitatem.
Item sanctum Iuonem ‡ iuris vtriusque doctorem presbyterumque et
confessorem de britania minori, qui fuit magne deuocionis et con-
templacionis atque miraculis claruit; ac semel cum missam celebraret
in eleuacione sacramenti visus est globius igneus super caput eius. 25
Item beatum lucensem siue lucencium § de podio bonai cuius capud
ego in manibus habui, et est in loco nostro qui est in tuscia super
montem imperialem, ubi est eciam corpus eius. Et monasterium
nostrum appellat[ur] sancti lucensis siue lucensii.§ Item produxit
sanctum lucium confessorem qui fuit primus sanctus de isto tercio 30
ordine Et sanctum Nicholucium de senis ac beatum Iacobum de laude
sacerdotem et miraculis clarum, Et beatum Petrum Romanum qui
sub soldano fuit | martirizatus, Sanctum bonazicum de vulterra, Et [Fol. 16ʳ]
beatum Petrum de colle, Ac beatum Alexandrum de perusio, Et

---

* MS. 'Kalender'. † Printed edit. 'servavit'.
‡ MS. 'Inonem'. § Printed edit. 'Luchesium, Luchesii'.

beatum leonem archiepiscopum Mediolani, Gualterium episcopum
triuisii, Et beatum Richardum episcopum fossombroni, Ac beatum
alexandrum magistrum theologie Et beatum Carolum * Ac beatum
Laudonem de monte feltro, Et beatum Iohannem de vrbino, Ac
5 beatum Iohannem de Rauena Et beatum torelum de pupio, Ac
beatum bartolum de sancto gemmano† Et beatum petrum pectinarium
de senis Ac beatum Robertum dominum arimini, Et beatum thoma-
succium de fulgenio prophetam ac miraculis clarissimum : similiter
quo ad mulieres produxit Sanctam elizabeth filiam regis hungarie
10 que fuit vxor landegauii ducis lothoringie. Item sanctam Rosam de
viterbio, Sanctam Margaretam de Cothona, Sanctam bonodonam de
bodio bona vxorem sancti luchesii, Beatam emilianam de florencia,
Et beatam Claram de monte falcie in cuius corde inuentus est
sculptus crucifixus cum omnibus misteriis passionis, & tres parue
15 pille in eius pectore reperte sunt quarum vna tantum ponderat
quantum due et quantum omnes tres simul. Et non plus ponderant
omnes tres simul quam vna sola : Per quod significatur quod ipsa
[Fol. 16ᵛ] habuit continuam memoriam passionis cristi et perfectam | fidem
vnitatis diuine essencie et equalitatis trium personarum diuinarum.
20 Que omnia Ego propriis oculis aspexi. Item beatam elizabeth im-
peratricem Romanorum vxorem caroli quarti regis francorum et
Imperatoris que miraculis coruscauit, Et beatam blancam reginam
francie, matrem sancti Ludouici regis francorum, que signis et
miraculis claruit, Et beatam meam de senis, Et beatam paschalinam
25 de fulgineo, Et beatam Michelinam de pensauro, Ac beatam angelam
de fulgineo que duodecim annis quotidie sumpsit dominicum corpus
[nihil] ‡ aliud manducans sed illo cibo celesti refecta oracioni et con-
templacioni vacabat. Item beatam beatricem de Rushonibus comi-
tissam que nostris temporibus fuit et a septem annis § citra mortua est
30 multisque miraculis claruit et est sepulta Mulier in ecclesia nostra
sancti angeli. Vt etiam dicit Magister bartholomeus pisanus vbi
supra Iste ordo commendari potest de nobilitate, Nam multi magni
homines de diuersis regnis christianitatis, Comites, Duces, principes,
barones & nobiles, tam viri quam mulieres, fuerunt de tercio ordine
[Fol. 17ʳ] beati Francissi. Inter quos vltra superius enarratos | fuit illa Regina
vngarie que fecit monasterium campi regis in austria Et alia regina
vngarie, mater regis ludouici ; istum quoque habitum induit quedam
Imperatrix Constantinopolis, Et vna regina cathalonie, Et rex Iacobus
dux sarbundie, & Magister magnifici Domini Iohannis Iacobi de
40 triulcio Et dominus Bartholomeus de vignate cuius proaui fuerunt
Domini ciuitatis laudensis. Et dominus lanzalotus de decio iuris

* MS. 'Caralum'.   † MS. 'gemmans'.
‡ MS. 'vel'.   § MS. 'annos'.

vtriusque doctor peritissimus ac lector in studio papiensi cum aliis
quasi in[n]umerabilibus * Et inbulla que incipit 'Sacri predicatorum
et minorum ordines'. que aurea appellatur concessit fratribus et
sororibus tercii ordinis et eorum congregacionum omnes gracias et
priuilegia que vnquam ipsis fratribus minoribus per sedem aposto- 5
licam sunt concessa dummodo eorum statui non repugnant, sicut
est predicare, Confessiones audire et huiusmodi. Et consequenter
gaudeant priuilegiis omnium fratrum mendicancium, sicut ipsi fratres
minores ut per eandem bullam patet per Sixt*u*m † pa*p*am quartum,
ut patet in parte secunda rosarii Bernardini de *b*usti ‡ Sermone 10
vicessimo septimo.

        * The quotation from Bernardine de Bustis ends here.
        † MS. 'Sixtam'.
        ‡ MS. 'Rusti'.

NOTES

¹ *Third order of Seynt Franceys . . . of the order of Penitentis.* This title is interesting as showing the earlier as well as the later name of the Tertiaries. From their foundation until nearly the end of the thirteenth century they were known in ecclesiastical documents and also popularly as *Fratres de Poenitentia* or *Ordo de Poenitentia*. It was not until the end of the thirteenth century that the title 'Third Order' was used as an official designation of the Franciscan Tertiaries. It will be noticed that the title, though appearing here in the heading, does not occur anywhere in the text of the Bull of Nicholas IV (1289). For full discussion of this topic see Mandonnet, *Les Règles et le gouvernement de l'Ordo de Pœnitentia au XIIIᵉ siècle*. Paris, 1902. Pp. 194–5.

² *Nicholas.* This is Nicholas IV (Hieronymus of Ascoli), a cardinal and Bishop of Palestrina. He was raised to the Pontificate on February 15, 1288, and occupied it until April 4, 1292. As stated at the end of this Bull, 1289 was the second year of his Pontificate. Nicholas was himself a Franciscan: he was indeed Minister General of the Order from 1274 to 1279.

³ *None heretike or suspect of heresy.* This clause indicates the fear which the Holy See entertained lest the new penitential 'fraternities', which were multiplying rapidly in the thirteenth century, might become heretical and a danger to the Church. Consisting largely of lay folk, they were constantly liable to drift into conflict with the hierarchy and even to lapse into heresy. *Or noysed thereupon*, Latin ' aut etiam infamatus '.

⁴ *After the cawcion of the pleggis.* A literal translation of the original 'secundum exhibitam pignoris cautionem'.

⁵ *Wᵗoute hem thought*, 'Unless it seems to them', i. e. to the ministers.

⁶ *Eny other approued religion.* The mediaeval use of the word 'religion' is more limited in sense than the modern use. It implies an organized branch of religion, a religious order.

⁷ *Price of the clothe.* This chapter shows the necessary development from the primitive simplicity of the early days. In R 1 it is prescribed that the price of the cloth must not exceed six 'solda' of Ravenna, a local measure which would obviously be useless for general use.

⁸ *Seint Martin lente*, often referred to as the lesser Lent, was the period from S. Martin's Day, November 11 until Christmas.

⁹ *Tyll seint Frauncys*, i. e. until the feast of S. Francis, October 4. For note on substitution of this feast for Michaelmas, see p. 32.

¹⁰ *Houseled* = 'communicated'.

¹¹ *Bearing of weapons.* This was one of the points which brought the 'Penitents' into collision with the secular authorities. They were thus prevented by the Rule from taking up arms in merely secular disputes. The creation of this Order and others with similar principles was one of the factors which contributed to the breakdown of Feudalism.

[12] *Matyns . . . Complyn.* These are the seven canonical hours, Matins, Prime, Terce, Sext, Nones, Vespers, and Compline. In the Latin text the 'hours' are enumerated in full.

[13] *Deus, in nomine tuo.* The opening words of Psalm liv.

[14] *Beati inmaculati.* The opening words of Psalm cxix.

[15] *Legem pone.* The opening words of verse 33 of Psalm cxix.

[16] *Crede,* that is the Apostles' Creed.

[17] *Miserere mei Deus,* i. e. Psalm li.

[18] *The great lent,* i. e. the Lent preceding Easter, in contradistinction to 'St. Martin's Lent' or 'the lesser Lent'.

[19] *Absteyne from solempne othes.* The provisions relating to the taking of oaths appear also in the Capestrano Rule and form one of many parallels with the Rule of the Humiliati. Whether there is a distinct reference here and in the corresponding chapters of R 1 to the Bull *Detestanda* is discussed on p. 29. R 2 and R 3 go further than R 1 in extending the circumstances for the taking of oaths 'for contractis of byeng and selling and of donacion', &c.

[20] *Here masse euery day.* In this respect R 3 is decidedly stricter than R 1; for under R 1 the Penitents were bound to hear Mass only once a month.

[21] *Storer.* Latin 'massarius' = treasurer.

[22] *Welthe* = well-being. Latin 'salute'.

[23] *Yf eny of them be incorrigible.* It will be noticed that the provisions relating to 'incorrigible brethren' appear twice, here in chap. xxiii and also in chap. xx.

[24] *Reate.* A town in Umbria lying between Assisi and Rome. It has many Franciscan associations.

[25] *XV Kalendes of Septembre* = August 18. For note on 'Kalender' see p. 37.

[26] *Seconde yere of oure pontificacion* = 1289. Nicholas IV ascended the Papal throne in 1288.

The Rewle
of
Sustris Menouresses enclosid

EDITED FROM A XV CENTURY MS.
(MS. Bodl. 585)
IN THE BODLEIAN LIBRARY

WITH AN

INTRODUCTION, NOTES, AND GLOSSARY

BY

WALTER W. SETON, M.A.

INTRODUCTION

THE ORDER OF S. CLARE.

THE connexion between the several branches of the great movement in the life of the Church, the Order of S. Francis, is so intimate and close that it is almost impossible to treat of any one branch of the Order without treating of the others. Most particularly is this the case when the Second Order or Order of S. Clare is considered. For while its history is interwoven with that of the Third Order or Order of Penitents, its history is quite inseparable from that of the First Order or Order of Friars Minor.

The Order of S. Clare has recently been the subject of much of the most valuable research which has been carried out in the field of Franciscan Studies. For the time being at any rate Père Livarius Oliger, O. F. M., has in his two articles in the *Archivum Franciscanum Historicum*,* '*De Origine Regularum Ordinis S. Clarae*,' so thoroughly and exhaustively reviewed both the materials and the criticism based upon them, that a restatement of the whole case is superfluous until new material comes to light. This does not imply that there are not some controversial points in Père Oliger's statement of the case, to certain of which reference will be made later. Again, Father Cuthbert's introduction to Mrs. Balfour's *Life and Legend of the Lady S. Clare* reviews very clearly one particular aspect of the Order, viz. the life-long struggle of S. Clare to keep alive the tradition of the early Franciscan spirit and to win for her whole spiritual family the Privilege of Poverty. Nor are these two works the only ones of importance in connexion with the story of the Clarisses. Much material will be found dealing with every aspect of the subject.

This being so, it appears unnecessary, in presenting an edition of the particular Rule of the Second Order which is here published, to

* Tom. v. Fasc. II and III. An. 1912.

restate in detail the facts already ascertained or to reargue the case. It will be sufficient to recapitulate very briefly the outstanding facts up to the year 1253 and then deal in greater detail with the so-called 'Isabella Rule'.

The birthday of the Order was Palm Sunday, 1212, when Clare left her home in Assisi and in the Chapel of the Portiuncula entered the religious life as a follower of S. Francis. In the following year she was placed by S. Francis in San Damiano together with a small band of sisters who had already followed her example. Whether there was a written Rule in existence between 1212 and 1218 is a disputed question, but at any rate no such Rule is at present known, and it would appear more probable that there was nothing more than a 'formula vitae' given to S. Clare by S. Francis, which is found quoted in the later Rule of 1253: *Quia divina inspiratione fecistis vos filias et ancillas altissimi summi Regis Patris coelestis, et Spiritui sancto vos desponsastis eligendo vivere secundum perfectionem sancti Evangelii: volo et promitto per me et Fratres meos semper habere de vobis tanquam de ipsis curam diligentem, et sollicitudinem specialem.*

This 'formula vitae' is important because it contains in embryo two of the most vital matters in the history of the Rule, viz. the 'evangelical perfection' or Privilege of Poverty and the dependence of the Clarisses upon the Friars Minor and their identification with the Franciscan Order.

The next fact of consequence is that in or about 1215 S. Clare obtained from the Pope Innocent III an oral grant of the so-called 'Privilege of Poverty'. It must here be explained what was the essential feature of the Privilege of Poverty as understood and practised by S. Francis and S. Clare. It did not mean merely that they personally and their followers individually renounced private property: that would have been no new feature, for it was one quite familiar in religious life. The essential feature was that property was not to be held by the community as a whole or as a corporate body: in other words, the community was to be dependent on the voluntary gifts of the faithful.

The first extant Rule of the Clarisses is what is generally known as the Hugoline Constitutions, so-called because they were drawn up in 1219 by Ugolino, Cardinal Bishop of Ostia, under authority granted to him by Honorius III. The text of the Hugoline

Introduction

Constitutions will be found in a Bull of Gregory IX.* The aim of these Constitutions was to bring the newly formed Order more directly under the authority of the Curia and to make it conform to a greater extent to the existing religious orders. But the Constitutions deliberately left out the Privilege of Poverty, and indeed made definite provision for property to be held in common and inherited by each house. It would seem that after the return of S. Francis from the East, Ugolino was persuaded by him to modify the Constitutions in the case of S. Clare's own house of San Damiano, outside Assisi, by recognizing the oral grant of poverty given to her by Innocent III, but this concession did not extend to the case of the other houses of the Clarisses.

The Hugoline Constitutions remained in force as the Rule of the Clarisses from 1219 to 1247, although it may be doubted whether they were ever really observed by the mother-house of San Damiano or indeed by certain other houses. The Papal records between those dates contain numerous Bulls relating to the Rule, some addressed to S. Clare and some to Blessed Agnes of Prague. It may here be mentioned that probably in the past too little attention has been paid to the part taken by Bl. Agnes in the negotiations with the Holy See as to the Privilege of Poverty.

The year 1247 was marked by the issue of a new Rule by Innocent IV, contained in the Bull *Cum omnis vera Religio*.† This Rule left the question of the Privilege of Poverty unaltered: there was still provision for the sisters to hold property in common for the use of the community. It marked progress, however, in this respect, namely, that it omitted the references to the Benedictine Rule, which had raised scruples in the minds of the Clarisses and of which more will be said later, and it defined their position as part of the Franciscan Order. Thus it provides that they are to live 'according to the Rule of Saint Francis so far as it relates to three things, obedience, surrender of private property, and chastity'. In the profession of the sisters the vow is made 'to God, and to Blessed Mary ever-Virgin, to *Blessed Francis* and all the Saints'. But, what is still more important, the care of all the houses of Clarisses is handed over to the Minister General and Provincials of the Order of Friars Minor. Such then was the second Rule of the Clarisses.

* Sbaralea, i. 263. † Sbar. i. 476.

66   *Introduction*

The year 1253 was that in which S. Clare's victory was won. Two days before her death, viz. on August 9 1253, Innocent IV issued the Bull *Solet annuere*,* which gave to the Order of Clarisses, not at San Damiano alone but everywhere, the long-coveted Privilege of Poverty. Neither the individual sisters nor the congregations were to be compelled to receive or inherit property.

S. Francis himself had died in 1226, i.e. twenty-seven years before the issue of this third Rule; thus during more than a quarter of a century S. Clare had stood fast for the primitive ideals which had governed S. Francis and which had led her in the beginning into the path of complete self-renunciation.

Before passing on from this point to the later history of the Rule which concerns more intimately the particular version here published, it is necessary to turn back and examine in somewhat greater detail one aspect of the question, viz. the significance of the references to the Benedictine Rule in the earlier versions of the Rule of the Clarisses.

Ever since the middle of the eighteenth century the question has been debated whether S. Clare at her profession adopted the Benedictine Rule, and whether and if so in what sense the Clarisses in the early history of the Order were Benedictines. Some of the outstanding facts are these:

The day following her profession S. Clare was committed by S. Francis to the Convent of S. Paulo near Bastia, which followed the Benedictine Rule, whence shortly afterwards she was transferred to another Benedictine House, S. Angeli de Panso on the slopes of Mount Subasio. It was not long, however, before she was brought to San Damiano, and there formed the community of Poor Ladies, living, as far as can be ascertained, in accordance with the 'formula vitae' given to her by S. Francis.

As has been seen, the first known form of the Rule of the Poor Ladies is found in the Hugoline Constitutions of 1218-19. Now these Constitutions contain the following words:

'Regulam Beatissimi Benedicti, in qua virtutum perfectio et summa discretio noscitur instituta, quae et a sanctis Patribus a principio devote suscepta est, et ab Ecclesia Romana venerabiliter approbata, vobis concedimus observandam in omnibus, in quibus eidem vivendi formulae vobis a Nobis traditae, cum adhuc essemus in minori officio constituti, contraria minime comprobatur.'

* Sbar. i. 671.

Introduction 67

These facts Père Oliger * explains by referring to the XIIIth Canon of the Lateran Council, which had been held in 1215 and which required that no new 'religion' should be founded in the Church, but that those who felt led to a religious vocation should attach themselves to one of the already existing Orders, e.g. the Benedictine or the Augustinian. As an illustration, he asserts that S. Dominic '*formaliter* Regulam S. Augustini accepit'. He infers that the references to the Benedictine Rule in the Hugoline Constitutions and in the later Bulls of the Holy See addressed to S. Clare must not be understood to imply that the Poor Ladies were regarded as following the Benedictine Rule otherwise than 'formaliter', that is as a kind of ecclesiastical fiction. It is of course quite true that Pope Innocent IV, writing to Bl. Agnes of Bohemia, had ruled that the obligation in respect of the Benedictine Rule implied no more than observance of the vows of canonical obedience, poverty, and chastity.† On the other hand it is clear that, whatever interpretation was put by the Curia upon the clauses requiring observance of the Benedictine Rule by the Poor Ladies, however much its significance was minimized by Innocent IV, the question was a very vital and acute one in the minds of the Poor Ladies themselves, at any rate at Prague. The Bull *In Divini timore nominis*, already mentioned, makes clear that it was issued because Bl. Agnes had written to the Pope, saying that the words in the Rule 'The Rule of S. Benedict', troubled their consciences, as they feared that by attempting to serve two Rules simultaneously they were committing mortal sin. Nor was this doubt confined to Bl. Agnes and her sisters at Prague. For in August, 1244, the Pope sent to S. Clare—whether in response to a remonstrance from her or not, we do not know—precisely the same ruling ‡ upon the words 'The Rule of S. Benedict' which he had sent in November, 1243, to Bl. Agnes. In November, 1245, the Hugoline Constitutions were reaffirmed in the Bull *Solet annuere* addressed to all the congregations of Poor Clares, and still the observance of the Benedictine Rule is required. Reference has already been made to the Rule of Innocent IV of 1247 § and to the fact that from this Rule

* *De Orig. Regul. Ordin. S. Clarae*, A. F. H., 1912, pp. 181-4, 203-5, 446-7.
† Bull *In Divini timore nominis*, Sbar. i. 242.
‡ Bull *Cum universitati vestrae*, Sbar. i. 350.
§ *Cum omnis vera Religio*, see p. 65.

the references to the Benedictine Rule disappear for the first time. That Rule was probably granted in response to representations made by S. Clare and Bl. Agnes, for the Pope refers to himself as being 'vestris piis precibus inclinati', and it may be supposed that one of the matters upon which they petitioned the Holy See—and this time successfully—was the elimination of the reference to the Benedictine Rule.

This repeated protest on the part of the Poor Ladies themselves and the tone of the responses from the Holy See make it difficult to accept Père Oliger's view that the observance of the Benedictine Rule by the Clarisses was a mere formality, and that it must not be understood as having constituted a real obligation; they make it hard to suppose that it is in any sense comparable with S. Dominic's relation to the Augustinian Rule. One illustration which Père Oliger himself gives seems to prove rather more than he intends it to show. He quotes the case of the Clarisses of Barcelona* who, in 1514, refused to be reformed, and contended that they were not Clarisses, but in reality Benedictines, giving as evidence for this the Bulls of Innocent IV, in which they were bidden to live after the Rule of the Holy Father Benedict; and ultimately they went over to the Benedictine Order. This may certainly show the confusion which arose in later years as to the Rules which governed individual Houses of Poor Clares, some of which had no desire to accept the settlement of 1253; but it also proves that the Benedictine character of the Hugoline Constitutions was something real as well as formal, if the Sisters at Barcelona were able thus successfully to appeal to the Hugoline Constitutions to show that they were Benedictines and not Franciscans. Special emphasis has been laid here on this matter as it is one of the few doubtful conclusions among those reached by Père Oliger in his otherwise most valuable treatise, which one must challenge.

The death of S. Clare in 1253 was an important event in the development of the Rule. With her passed away one of the last direct links between her Order and the great Founder. It is true that her tradition was carried on for more than a quarter of a century after her death by her friend and correspondent, Bl. Agnes, who died in 1281/82. But the years which followed 1253 were marked by a falling away from the ideals of S. Clare in the Order

* Annibal de Latera. *Suppl. ad Bull.* Rome, 1780, part ii. 60.

Introduction 69

generally, rather than by the development of them further. Taking then 1253 as a fresh starting-point, we find the Rule formulated in exact accordance with the life-long desires of S. Clare; the Privilege of Poverty duly granted and acknowledged; the Clarisses occupying their spiritual birthright as part of the Order of S. Francis. But it may well be doubted whether all the Houses of Poor Clares were imbued with the fervent spirit of the mother-house.

The next stage in the history of the Rule centres around a new House, which did not regard the Privilege of Poverty as an essential feature of its loyalty to S. Clare. It was in 1254 or 1255 that Blessed Isabella, sister of S. Louis, King of France, founded in the Diocese of Paris the Monastery of Longchamp, known more generally as 'Abbatia Humilitatis Beatae Mariae'. The first stone was laid by S. Louis himself on June 10, 1256. For this new House, Isabella did not desire to adopt any one of the existing Rules of the Clarisses, but her plan was to secure the Papal approbation for a new Rule which was to be an amalgam of previous Rules. To her the absolute poverty which was sought after by S. Clare was too hard a path; she was content that the sisters of Longchamp should hold property, which was to be administered for them by a Procurator according to the provision made by the Rule of 1247. On the other hand, she desired to incorporate provisions making clear their lineal connexion with the Franciscans and placing them under the direction of the Minister General and the Provincials of the Friars Minor. A life of Bl. Isabella by Agnes de Harcourt tells us that the new Rule was drawn up by five of the Friars Minor who were learned masters of theology. The names given by Agnes de Harcourt are: *Frater Bonaventura, frater Guilielmus de Milletonne, frater Odo de Roni, frater Godefridus de Vierson, frater Guilielmus de Harcombour.*

According to Père Oliger this Rule was approved by Alexander IV: later, namely on July 27, 1263, it was confirmed with some alterations by Urban IV in the Bull *Religionis augmentum.*[*] Still later, the Rule thus prepared under the supervision of Bl. Isabella was slightly modified by Boniface VIII, and it is the English version of this Rule as revised by Boniface VIII which is here published.

* Sbar. ii. 477.

It was for some time believed that the text of the Rule as originally approved by Alexander IV was no longer in existence. That was the view expressed by Sbaralea in his publication of vol. ii of the *Bullarium Franciscanum* in which *Religionis augmentum* is contained. The same view has been quite recently repeated by Père Oliger, who in his work already mentioned, writes:

Opus quinque Magistrorum primum approbatum est ab Alexandro IV, cuius tamen diploma non superest.

Père Oliger appears to have overlooked the fact that Sbaralea himself had by the time he published his third volume discovered an original autograph copy of the Bull of Alexander IV with the leaden seal in the Archives of the Convent of Holy Cross, Florence: the Bull, which is dated February 2, 1259, has the following ending:

Explicit Regula Humilium Ancillarum Gloriosissimae Mariae Virginis Matris Dei, quam Frater Mansuetus de Ordine Fratrum Minorum de mandato Summi Pontificis et Cardinalium quorumdam diligenti consilio composuit et dictavit.

Now the name of Frater Mansuetus does not occur among the names of the five masters of theology who, according to Agnes of Harcourt, prepared the Rule. Further, Agnes states:

Prae ceteris volebat ut sorores abbatiae nominarentur 'sorores minores', neque ullo modo Regula illi sufficere poterat, nisi istud nomen illi fuisset insertum.

Now the name *sorores minores* is precisely one of the alterations made by Urban's Bull *Religionis augmentum* upon the work of Alexander IV.

'And we ordeynid and establissin þat þis rule be clepid from þis time forþe Menoressis enclosid.' *; whereas in the Bull of Alexander IV the name *Sorores Minores* does not occur and the sisters are called *Sorores Ordinis Humilium Ancillarum Beatissimae Virginis Gloriosae.* The inference is obvious. The Bull approved by Alexander IV in 1259 is anterior to the one composed by the five Masters of Theology, and was probably composed not by them, but by one Frater Mansuetus by the direction of the Pope. It must be, however, admitted that the only evidence for this theory is the unique copy of the Bull mentioned by Sbaralea and

* See p. 81, l. 26.

reprinted also by Flaminius Annibal in his Supplement to the Bullarium.

The first sisters of the Monastery of Longchamp came apparently from the House of San Damiano at Rheims, as is shown by a Bull of Alexander IV dated from Anagnia, February 12, 1259, i.e. just ten days before the Bull which first approved the Isabella Rule. It appears that the Isabella Rule never had a very great vogue outside France. It was soon superseded to a great extent by the Urbanist Rule of 1263. Père Oliger refers to only one House in Italy adopting this Rule, and he makes no reference at all to the English colony which will be described later. There is, however, one other House, following the Isabella Rule, which has an interesting link with the manuscript here published, and that is the Monastery of S. Catherine of Provence. A Bull of Urban IV, dated June 22, 1264, states in the preamble that the Rule granted by Alexander IV to Longchamp had been revised by Cardinal Simon de Bria, and that he (Urban) was moved to this revision by the King of Navarre (*Carissimi in Christo filii nostri Regis Navarre illustris precibus inclinati*). This King of Navarre was Henry III, who died in 1270, and was the first husband of Blanche, whose part in bringing the Clarisses to London will appear later.

In order to complete this brief sketch of the development of the Rule of the Clarisses, reference must be made to the final Rule, which also was issued by Urban IV in 1263. The Bull *Beata Clara** of October 18, 1263, approved a new Rule written by Cardinal Caietanus, the Protector of the Order. The new Rule is to a large extent a compilation based on the previous Rules, and among other innovations it abolishes the various names by which the Sisters had come in process of time to be known, and gives to the whole Order the name of the 'Order of S. Clare'.

This Rule became the final and authoritative Rule, and has not since then been superseded.

THE ENGLISH VERSION OF THE RULE.

The English version of the Rule of the Second Order or 'Menouresses enclosid' is contained in MS. Bodl. 585 = 2357 in the Bodleian Library. The volume, which consists of 104 leaves of

* Sbar. ii. 509.

parchment, is made up of two separate MSS. bound together. Both MSS. were apparently written in England in the fifteenth century.

The first MS. in the volume is in Latin, and contains:

Fol. 1ʳ–17ᵛ. *Tractatus de vita et nobilitate et marturio sanctorum Albani et Amphibali de quodam libro gallico excerptus et in latinum translatus.*

Fol. 18ᵛ–47ʳ. *De Granario magistri Iohannis Wetanstede.*

At folio 48ʳ the second MS. begins. It is written in English in a neat and legible book-hand.

Fol. 48ʳ–72ʳ contain the Rule of the Clarisses which is here published. It is divided into chapters or sections of varied length, and each chapter is begun with a finely illuminated Capital. There are no other illuminations, and otherwise the writing is entirely in black.

Following immediately after the Rule, and contained in folios 72ʳ–101ʳ, is a treatise by the same hand, and clearly forming part of the same Manuscript, consisting of instructions relating to the ordering of the services.

The Manuscript measures 219 mm. by 143 mm., and is bound in limp vellum.

The Catalogue* gives the information that the second MS. was presented to the Bodleian Library by Charles Howard, Earl of Nottingham, in 1604.

Fortunately it is possible to determine practically with certainty the particular convent for which this MS. was written.

The Rule which it contains is, as has already been stated, substantially the Rule of Blessed Isabella of 1263. The fact that the language of this version is English indicates that it was written for use in an English convent. The fact that it is the Isabella Rule and not the ordinary Urbanist Rule (also of 1263) would lead us to expect that it would belong to a daughter-house of the Monastery of Longchamp in the Diocese of Paris.

The opening words of the Rule are sufficient in themselves to establish the connexion with this celebrated religious house.

The house in question is none other than the former convent of

---

* *Summary Catalogue of Western MSS. in the Bodleian Library*, by F. Madan and H. H. E. Craster, 1912

Clarisses or 'Minoressis' just outside the walls of the City of London, near Aldgate, in the street now known as 'Minories'. A very full account of the house, its foundation, history, and ultimate dissolution, is contained in a paper read by Dr. Fly befoi e the Society of Antiquaries, June 23, 1803.* An account is also given in Dugdale's *Monasticon Anglicanum* under the general heading of Franciscans in England, and also in Tanner's *Notitia Monastica*. A more modern account will be found in the *Victoria History of London* (1909), edited by William Page, vol. i, pp. 516-19.

It has generally been held the first colony of Clarisses was brought over to England from the Diocese of Paris from Longchamp by Blanche, widow of the King of Navarre, and, later, wife of Edmund, Duke of Lancaster, brother of King Edward I. She was the daughter of Robert, Count d'Artois and Maud of Brabant. The earliest record relating to this colony of Clarisses is a charter of Edward I authorizing his brother Edmund to convey a parcel of land given by Thomas de Bredstrete in the parish of S. Botolph outside Aldgate:

dilectis nobis in Christo monialibus de ordine Minorum, quae per nobilem dominam Blancam reginam Navarrae, consortem eiusdem fratris nostri, in Angliam sunt venturae, et infra regnum nostrum moraturae, ac Deo et beatae Mariae ac beato Francisco servituraе.†

This document is dated from Westminster, June 28, 1293, and shows that at that time the Sisters were about to arrive, but had not done so.

There is, however, some reason to suppose that the Convent was in existence at least twelve years earlier. Sbaralea gives a Bull of Martin IV *Loca Sanctorum omnium*,‡ dated October 9, 1281, addressed to all the Faithful and granting an indulgence of one hundred days to those visiting this church (among others) on the Sunday after Ascension Day and its Octave. As this was a somewhat exceptional privilege, it seems improbable that it would have been conferred on the church immediately after its founda-

---

* *Archaeologia*, vol. xv, section viii, pp. 92-113.
† *Monumenta Franciscana*, ed. Brewer (Rolls Series), Appendix xxviii, p. 625.
‡ Sbar. iv. 339.

Introduction

tion, and so probably both Church and Convent were in existence a good deal earlier than 1281. Moreover, the House is mentioned in the Taxatio of Pope Nicholas about 1291.*

The first Abbess of the English house was, according to Dr. Fly, Isabella de Lille and the second Joanne de Nevers, both French names, which are a further indication of the French parentage of the 'Minories'.

Six Papal Bulls are extant relating to the Convent of the Minories, up to and including the reign of Boniface VIII.

The first is dated September 13, 1294,† and reminds the Sisters of certain privileges to which they were entitled, and of which apparently they were not availing themselves.

The other five belong to the reign of Boniface VIII.

The second, *Vestrae religionis* ‡ of April 6, 1295, grants to the 'Minoressis' a church which is in the patronage of Edmund, brother of the King, subject to the reservation of a portion of its income for the support of the vicar.

The third, dated July 3, 1295,§ confines the convent to the 'inclosid Minoresses' who observe the Rule that prevails in the monastery of the Humility of S. Mary in the Diocese of Paris.

The fourth, *Romana Ecclesia*, dated August 31, 1295, places the Convent under the direct jurisdiction of the Roman See, and removes it from that of the Bishop of London.‖

The fifth, *Religiosam vitam*,¶ dated March 13, 1296, commands that the Sisters are to be protected, and confirms their privileges and possessions.

The sixth, *Petitio vestra*,** dated March 3, 1298, gives the Minoressis permission to take possession of the church of Hertindon,

---

* *Victoria History of London*, ed. W. Page, vol. i, p. 516.

† Dr. Fly and, following him, the later editions of Dugdale attribute this Bull to Boniface VIII, in spite of the date: but Boniface did not become Pope until December 1294. I have been unable to trace this Bull in Potthast or Sbaralea. If it is rightly dated, it must belong to the reign of Celestine V.

‡ Sbar. Suppl. p. 203. Potthast, 24056.

§ This is apparently the same as the Bull given by Potthast, *Laudabilis sacra religio* 24359, which is a re-issue of an earlier Bull (Pott. 24346) addressed to all Houses of Clarisses, relieving them of the obligation of tenths.

‖ Sbar. iv. 365. Potthast, 24176. Both Dr. Fly and *The Victoria Hist. of London* inaccurately assign this Bull to August 1294, when Boniface VIII was not yet Pope.

¶ Sbar. iv. 385. Potthast, 24297. ** Sbar. iv. 462. Potthast, 24631.

of which Edmund was patron, notwithstanding the fact that the revenues of that church exceeded 40 marks a year.

The Bodleian MS. makes clear that the Rule used in the London Convent was the Isabella Rule, but in some details revised by Boniface VIII. It will be observed, for example, on fol. 52ʳ (p. 84), that in the vow of profession the sister undertakes 'to lyve after þe rule of myne lorde þe apostle Boneface þe eytiþ correctid and approuid', whereas in the Rule as issued in 1263 she undertook to live according to 'the rule granted to our order by the Lord Pope Alexander IV and corrected and approved by the Lord Pope Urban IV'. Again, in the Appendix to the Rule on fol. 75ᵛ (p. 100) the following sentence occurs:

'And ȝit as we recordin oure blessid predecessoures pope boneface þe VIII þat after a constitucioun bi hem ordeynid vppon þis same religioun vnder vertuous rule, þat alle the Sustris schulden dwelle and abide vnder stedefaste and perpetuel closinge,' &c.

In this sentence the word 'pope' is rubbed out, and the words 'boneface þe VIII' are crossed through.

Another document relating to the 'Minories' belongs to the year 1296, when King Edward I confirms a grant of ten acres of land *de dominico suo in campo de Hertindon in comitatu Derbiae* made by his brother Edmund to *dilectis nobis in Christo abbatissae de gratia Beatae Mariae ordinis Sanctae Clarae extra muros Londoniae et eiusdem loci sororibus Deo ibidem servientibus.*

The house was surrendered to Henry VIII by Elizabeth Savage, the last Abbess, in 1539,* and in 1540 the site was granted by the King to the Bishop of Bath and Wells. It appears, however, at a later date to have reverted to the Crown. In 1797, according to Dugdale, a fire took place in the neighbourhood which exposed to view larger remains of the conventual offices than had before been visible.

So far, then, as the history of the Bodleian MS. is concerned, it appears probable that it remained in the Convent of the Minories until its dissolution in 1539. Reference has already been made to the fact that the Manuscript was presented to the Bodleian Library in 1604 by Charles Howard, Earl of Nottingham. Now it appears, from information courteously supplied by the authorities of the Bodleian Library, that Charles Howard presented

---

* *Wriothesley*, Camden Soc. i. 94.

also sixteen other MSS. and thirty-four printed books; of the seventeen MSS., all except five can be proved to have come from the Library of King Henry VIII, and MS. Bodl. 585 is among these five. Other sources from which Charles Howard's books came are the Libraries of Cranmer, of Sir Thomas Coppley, and of William Devenishe, but there is nothing to connect MS. Bodl. 585 with any one of these. On the whole, it would appear probable that the MS. came, like the majority of Charles Howard's MSS., from the Library of King Henry VIII. It may accordingly be reasonably supposed that the MSS. of the Convent of the Minories passed into the hands of the King in 1539 at its dissolution.

There is further evidence that the MS. remained in conventual hands until the dissolution. In every case where the words 'pope' or 'papal' occur in the MS. they have been either erased or crossed through with a pen. It is known that about 1536 the King issued an order requiring such erasures to be made in the service-books and other MSS. in the possession of religious houses. Gairdner* gives an interesting illustration of the way in which this order was received. Sir William Sherbourne, the parish priest of Woburn Chapel, was rebuked by the Abbot, Robert Hobbes, for using a knife to rase the Pope's name, telling him to do it with a pen, for 'it will come again one day'. The following year (1538) the said Abbot was hanged on an oak-tree before the gate of his own Abbey. The erasures made so thoroughly in MS. Bodl. 585 point to the fact that it was in 1536-7 in the hands of its original owners, who executed the royal command. It is interesting to note that in cases where the word 'apostle' is used as referring to the Pope, the word is not erased, probably because it was misunderstood.

An examination of the English version shows that it is probably a translation from a French version of the original Latin, and, moreover, by no means a good translation. Throughout, the translator slavishly follows the original text, both in the construction of the sentences and in the choice of words. In many cases it is quite clear that the translator has entirely failed to understand the original, and consequently the English makes no sense. In editing the text, where the sense can be rectified by the addition

* *Lollardy and the Reformation in England*, vol. ii, p. 135.

or alteration of a word or two (e.g. sometimes by the addition of a negative!), this has been done; but in cases where the sense cannot be restored without entirely rewriting the sentence, it has been deemed best to leave it uncorrected and to give the Latin text in the notes. This applies, in particular, to the first six folios, which are especially bad.

It remains to say something in conclusion about the material which forms an Appendix to the Rule in the Bodleian MS. It follows on to the Rule itself without a break, and is in the same hand as the Rule. It will, however, readily be seen that it is not one document, but a compilation of two or more documents. The first part, from fol. 72ᵛ to fol. 78ᵛ (to 'wiþowte any variaunce or lettinge') is clearly a Papal document; it would appear to be a portion of a Bull containing a confirmation of the Rule and some modifications of its practice. It contains some material which also forms part of the Rule itself in other words. The reference to 'pope boneface þe viii' on fol. 75ᵛ as a predecessor may suggest that this Bull was the work of Benedict X, but it does not necessarily follow that the immediate predecessor is meant. No Bull containing this material is found either in Potthast or in Sbaralea's *Bullarium Franciscanum*. The material beginning on fol. 78ᵛ: 'At alle þe houres', is not in the form of a Papal Bull, and consists of regulations setting out the practice of the Convent. Towards the end, viz. on fol. 100ᵛ, it drifts into the first person narrative. 'We make vtas of Noel'; the same happens earlier on fol. 80ᵛ 'til we sey *Fidelium animae*', but in the context this looks like a slip for 'þey'. There is, at present, no further evidence as to the authorship or provenance of the material forming the Appendix.

The Editor wishes to record his great indebtedness to Mr. A. G. Little, Chairman of the British Society of Franciscan Studies, who called his attention to the Bodleian MS.; to Dr. R. W. Chambers, who has given much help in revising the text; and to Mrs. Geoffrey Tomes, who made the transcript of the text from the MS. with great skill and accuracy.

BIBLIOGRAPHY

Berguin. La Bienheureuse Isabelle de France. Grenoble, 1899.
Brewer, J. S. Monumenta Franciscana. (Rolls Series.) Appendices xxv, xxvii, xxviii, pp. 622–6.
Cozza-Luzi. Chiara di Assisi secondo alcune nuove scoperte e documenti. Rome, 1895.
Cuthbert, Father. Introduction to Mrs. Balfour's *Life and Legend of the Lady Saint Clare*. London, 1910.
Cuthbert, Father. Life of Saint Francis of Assisi. Book ii, chapter iv. London, 1912.
Duchesne, H. Gaston. Histoire de l'Abbaye Royale de Longchamps. Paris, 1906.
Fly, Dr. Article in Archaeologia, vol. xv, section viii, pp. 92–113. London, 1803.
Goffin. La Vie et Légende de Madame Saincte Claire. Paris, 1907.
Heimbucher, Max. Die Orden und Kongregationen der katholischen Kirche. Paderborn, 1902. Vol. 2, pp. 475–89.
Jörgensen, J. Saint Francis of Assisi: A Biography. Book II, chapter v. London, 1912.
Lemmens, Fr. Die Anfänge des Klarissenordens. Römische Quartalschrift, t. xvi, p. 97 ff.
Lempp, E. Die Anfänge des Klarissenordens. Zeit. für Kirchengeschichte, t. xxiii, pp. 626–9.
Locatelli. Ste Claire d'Assise. Rome, 1899–1900.
Oliger, Père Livarius. De Origine Regularum Ordinis S. Clarae. Archivum Franciscanum Historicum. Tom. v. Fasc. II and III. An. 1912. (Quaracchi.)
Pennacchi, F. Legenda Sanctae Clarae Virginis. Assisi, 1910.
Robinson, Father Paschal. Life of Saint Clare. 1910.
Robinson, Father Paschal. The Rule of St. Clare and its Observance in the Light of Early Documents. Philadelphia, 1912.
Robinson, Father Paschal. The Writings of St. Clare of Assisi. Archivum Franc. Histor. Tom. III. Fasc. III. An. 1910. Quaracchi.
Sbaralea. Bullarium Franciscanum, 1759: with supplement of Flaminius Annibal, 1780.
Seraphicae Legislationis Textus Originales, p. 74 ff. and p. 274 ff. (For the Rule and Testament of S. Clare.) Quaracchi, 1897.
Wauer, E. Entstehung und Ausbreitung des Klarissenordens. Leipzig, 1906.

THE REWLE OF
SUSTRIS MENOURESSES ENCLOSID

[*Note*—The Reader is referred to the note on p. 44 for an explanation of the practice with respect to contractions, italics, and brackets in this text.]

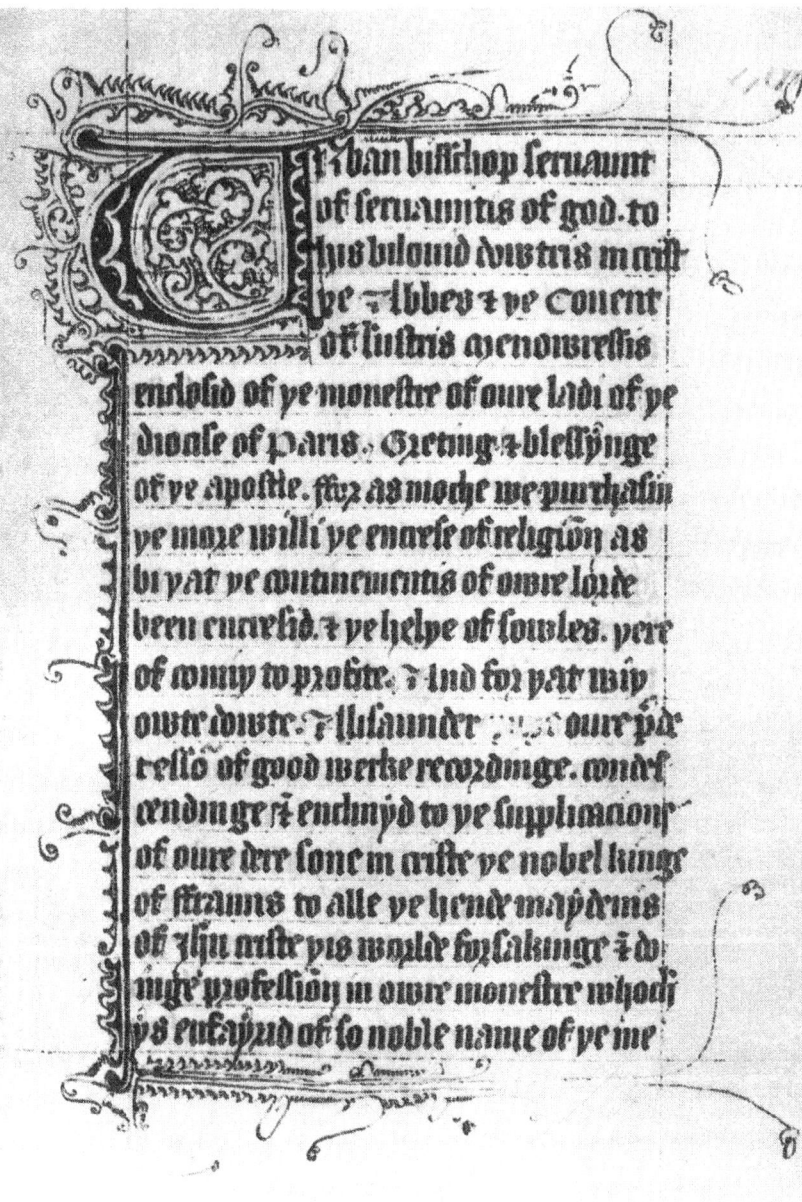

FOLIO 48 r. OF MS. BODL. 585.

THE REWLE OF SUSTRIS MENOURESSES ENCLOSID

URban [1] * bisschop seruaunt of seruauntis of god, to his bilouid [Fol. 48ʳ] dowtris in crist, þe Abbes & þe couent of sustris Menowressis enclosid of þe monestre of oure ladi of þe diocise of Paris, Greting & blessynge of þe apostle. For as moche we purchasin þe more willi[*nglye*]þe encrese of religioun, as bi þat þe continementis of owre 5 lorde been encresid, & þe helþe of sowles þereof comiþ to profite; And for þat wiþowte dowte, Alisaunder [2] pope † oure predecessour of good werke recordinge, condescendinge & enclinyd to þe supplicacions of oure dere sone in criste þe nobel kinge of Frauns [3], to alle þe hende maydenis of Ihesu criste þis worlde forsakinge & doinge 10 professioun in owre monestre [4] whoche ys enfayrid of so noble name of þe me|kenesse of blessid marie, þe whoche Minster whan hit was [Fol. 48ᵛ] nyew made none body þer was dwellinge, as hit is sayde, grauntid þe rule whoche ys writyn here after for to holde & kepe perpetueli in þe same mynster, and beene clepid bi þe name of sustris enclosid [5]. 15 And werevpon alle [6] Hit was to us prayde lowli bi þe same kyng that [*we*] þe forseyde rewle in some chapitres diden amende, & þat [*we*] ‡ schulden take bysines, þorw beningnite of apostle to put to at þe schewinge of þis rewle þe name of meneres. And than [*we*] § enclinid to þe preyeres of þe same kynge, þe same rule by owre 20 louid sonne Symon Deutre [7] preest Cardinal of þe title of seynt Cecile did amende, so þat it was ‖ done as it was in name [8]. But nameli þat ye same mynster, as hit is aboue sette, haue worschippid þe house of humilite of oure | ladi & þat þis rewle may be fayrid bi [Fol. 49ʳ] þe profitȝ of þe same humilite, to þe name of þe sayde rule, we 25 sette to þe forseyde name of menours. And we ordeynid & establissin [9] þat þis rule be clepid from þis time forþe, Menoressis enclosid, & þat it be kept perpetuali in þe same mynster & in other minsteris whoche schal be fownded here after or plantid, In þe

---

* The numbers given in the text refer to the notes which will be found on pages 117-19.
      † Word erased, but legible.   ‡ MS. 'þey'.
    § MS. later hand, 'þey' over an erasure.   ‖ Word erased before 'done'.

G

whiche þe same sustris schal make professioun to þis reddure, as it
is amendid. The whoche rule & þe life of þis same sustris enclosid
we haue do notefiyd here after, þe whiche is þis.

 Eche womman whiche bi þe grace & gifte of þe holi goste schal
5 be brouht to entre in þis ordre for to nyȝe to god owre lorde Ihesu
Criste & to his ful swete moder, after þe cownsayle of þe perfeccioun
[Fol. 49ᵛ] of þe gospel, Lyue alle dayes in obediens, & chas|tite, wiþowte
properte, And for to dwelle alle dayes of her life enclosid as a
tresoure kepte to þe souereyne kynge.

10 Alle þo whoche schal leuen þe vanite of þe worlde & in to þe
forseyde abbey schal comen, þis religioun for to resseyue, schal kepe
bysili þis maner of lyuinge alle here life, after þat time þat þey
been professid, & been bowndin be obediens for to dwelle enclosid
wiþ in þe cloyster of þe abbey, But ȝif so be [10] þat sche haue en-
15 special conge of þe [pope *] or of þe general mynistre of þe ordre
of Frere menowris or of þe prouincial of þe same prouince in þe
whiche þe same Abbey is foundid, & þat bi cause for to edefie, or to
plante þe same religioun, or for cause of gouernauns of somme place
of þe forseyde religioun, Some haue been sent in to oþer places, þe |
[Fol. 50ʳ] whoche haue bihouyd afterwarde to returne to þe same places from
whoche þey comyn bi þe licence of one of hem forseyde, ȝif hit seme
good & expedient to þe Mynistre or to one of hem for to do. And
ȝif hit happe so be werre, or be water, or be fire, or for oþer like
case þat þe same Abbey falle to be destruyid or þat it be like þat
25 þe hous schal falle downe or for drede of enemyes, þey were putte
in soche verray & experte informacioun, þat wiþ oute greuous peril &
opun destruxioun none bodi may dwelle ne abide þere, for to haue þe
counsayle & þe conge of þe Mynster, þat þan bi þe counsayle & con-
sentement of alle couent & bi þe comaundement of þe Abbes, þe
30 Sustris þer may leueli remew þennis in to anoþer place sure, where
[Fol. 50ᵛ] þat þey may dwelle honest|li & saueli enclosid vntil þe time þat it
schal be oþer weyes wiseli ordeynid for hem what þat þey schul doo.
And ȝif þe coueut bi any cause resonable here Abbey oþer place
edifi, þan þe sustryn bi licence of þe Ministre general may remuyn
35 in to anoþer place couenable.

     * Word deleted in MS.

The Rewle of Sustris Menouresses enclosid

Alle þe Nonnes þer which happin for to dyȝe þer professid or nouices or sustris or seruauntis schal be byriyd wiþinne þe cloyster of þe abbey. Alle þoo whoche þis religioun schal take in þe forseyde Abbey & in oþer whoche of nyew schal be foundid, to þe whoche þis noble rule schal be grauntid & holdin, bifore þat þey haue here 5 abite & þat þey schul enter into religioun, þat it be wel declarid to hem þe hardnessis & þe scharpenessis by whoche þey comiþ to Ioye of Paradise, & þese whiche þey schullen be bown|dyn to after þis [Fol. 51ʳ] religioun.

None womman schal be resseyuyd, woche for age or for sikenesse 10 or for fole simplesse[11] after þe iugement of hem whoche haue for to do þer of, be nat couena[b]le & suffisaunt for to kepe þe maner of life, & also bi any oþer[12] auenture, þat þan in oþer place bi counsel of þe most wise susteris of þe place, be for þe forseyde Ministre or one of hem dispense to another soche & þat bi cause 15 resonable.

Alle þo þat wolen in þis holi abbey abiden & in ani oþer whoche schal be fowndid here after, to þe whoche þis rule schal be grauntid & holden, And * þat wole þis holi religioun resseyue, allegatis forsake prides & vaniteis of þis schort life . And as þey schul be 20 resseyuid wiþ in þe cloy|ster, abide þey þere, & as sone as þey [Fol. 51ᵛ] schullen be schorne, þey schullin leue þe robis of þe worlde. Thanne a wise maystresse & moste deuowte sustre in þe Abbey be ordeyned & be I-take to hem for to exite hem to holinesse & to holi vertues & for to speke to hem in feruent deuocioun & also for to 25 teche hem for to abide & bere † hem in swetnesse of charite in alle poyntes whoche longin to holi religioun & bisili for to repreue hem of alle þinges whoche been repreueable. And þat þey be nat suffrid to entre in to þe chapitre duringe þe ȝere, but ȝif so be þat it be for cause of amonissinge & repreuinge. The ȝere fulfillid, make þey pro- 30 fessioun in hondes of þe Abbesse bifore alle þe couent in þis manere. 'I Suster ... ‡ bihote to god & owre ladi blissid mayde marie & to |

* MS. adds 'sche', which is superfluous. † MS. 'here'. ‡ No gap in MS.

[Fol. 52ʳ] seynt Fraunces, to myne ladi seint Clare'³ & to alle seyntis, in ʒoure hondes, moder, to lyue after þe rule * of myne lorde þe apostle Boneface þe eytiþ¹⁴ correctid & approuid be alle þe time of myne life, In obedience, In chastite, wiþowte properte or voyse in þe Cloyster, After þat whoche is ordeynid bi þe same Rule in alle poyntis.'

This like maner to make professioun holdyn þey whoche been ordeyned to serue & seche. Suche schulyn [nat] goo owte of þe Abbey, But alweyis ʒif hit happe be any riht & necessari cause for to sende owte of þe cloyster hem whiche servyn & been professid, In þe same maner bi leue of þe ministre general, Soche algatis be sent whoche been honeste & demurid in vertues & in age. Þe whiche whan þey schul so go oute of þe Cloyster, þey schul be [Fol. 52ᵛ] ho|sid & schod beringe none cordis¹⁵ & þey schulle nat go alone.

ECche suster schal be cloþid in stamyn or heyre & ʒif here likiþ, sche may haue two cotis or þre or foure, after þat as it schal beste lyke to þe Abbesse, euermore eschuynge þe owtrage of cloþes & of robis in gode maner, Soo þat sche haue a mantel or tweyne couenable longe & brode . These robis schullen be of buystouse cloþe & low prise & of pouer coloure . And sche schal nat vse here ouereste cote¹⁶ alle white ne alle blacke. Þes sustris, after þey been professid, þey schul use bifore gerdellis cordes whiche shal be made wiþ coriouste¹⁷. And þey schul usyn kerchiues honestli in one maner of kerchiues & of colleres, whoche schal be alle white & nat | [Fol. 53ʳ] precious. And also þat þe forhede & þe yʒen been couerid, as it bihouiþ, & in none oþer maner be þey nat so hardi for to apere bifore strawngeris ; for it falliþ nat to hem whoche ys weddid to þe kynge perpetuel þat sche chiere none oþer but him, ne delite her in none oþer but in him. And also þat þey haue a blacke veyle I-spred aboue her hedis so large & so longe, þat hit may stretche from eche parti to þe schuldris & behinde at þe backe resonabli, wiþowte whiche þey schul mow be on nytes & some time on dayes bi licence of þe abbesse. Alle þese þinges þe forseyde sustris schullin haue & kepe, And þey whoche seruyn & whoche been or-

* The words ' of myne lorde þe apostle Boneface þe eytiþ' are underlined in MS.

deyneid nat for to passe oute. But oþer seruauntes & nouicis schullin haue gerdellis of wolle & white veylis on here hedis. The abbesse schal ordeyne, after þat sche schal best se for | to do, of [Fol. 53ᵛ] chausures for þe sustris & to hem whoche seruyn wiþ inne þe cloyster.

The Abbesse & alle sustres hole & alle oþer schullen lye in þe comune dortre & eche bi here selue haue a bed disseuerid fram oþer. The bedde for þe abbesse be made in soche place of þe dortoure þat sche may se [*fram*] here bed, ȝif it may be couenably, alle oþer beddis of þe dortoure wiþoute any stoppynge; & þat be alle 10 nyhte in þe dortoure bi clere & continuel liht. From þe resurrexioun of oure lorde til þe Fest of þe Natiuite of oure ladi,[18] after mete til þe houre of none þe sustris schulle slepe, þey þat willen; & þey þat nille nat slepen, ocupie hem in preyeres & þowtes of god or in oþer pesibel & gode trauayles. Eche may haue a sacke 15 I-fillid wiþ strawe or wiþ hey, oþer ellis a cowche in stede of a sacke & a wol|lin cloþe buystus I-spred aboue & a cusschin I-couerid [Fol. 54ʳ] wiþ linnyn cloþe, I-stoppid wiþ hey or strawe or grete wolle or federis, like as þe abbesse schal ordeyne; & þat þey haue couertoures wiþoute skynnes wher wiþ þey may couer hem, But bi 20 licence of þe Abbesse þo þat been syke may haue couertoures wiþ skynnes. Alle þe sustres schal haue here heris rowndid or alle clippid & þat at certeyne tyme to here eris.

FOr to do þe office & seruise of god by day & be nyht to þe preysing of god & to þe gladnes of his glorie, The sustris schul 25 haue hem & gouerne hem, as it is writen here after.

Þe sustres whoche canne rede & singe schal do þe office reuerentli & mesurabli after þe custome & þe ordre of freris menoures, & þe oþer schal sey xx [19] *Pater noster* | for matyns, v for laudis; For [Fol. 54 b] prime, tierce, sexte, none, & complin, For eche owre vii *Pater* 30 *noster*, And for euynsonge, xii *Pater noster*. And in þis same maner be alle þinges in þe office of oure blissid ladi; be hit kepte wiþ deuowte preyinge for þe dede. And ȝif þer be any sustris couenable & of gode witte, The abbes, ȝif sche þenkiþ hem goode, to ordeyne & assigne a maystresse couenable & honeste for to teche 35 hem songe, to performe þe office & seruise of god stedfastli. The sustris & þey whiche servyn in werkis & placis stabelliche, be hit ordeynid þat þey schul been ocupiid in profitable & honest trauayles, bi þe whiche maner þat slowþe & schlugri whoche been grete enemyes continueli to þe sowle * schal be skerid awey & [Fol. 55ʳ] eschewid, þat it lette nat ne stawnche | nat þe spirit of preyere & deuocioun, to whom alle oþer wordli þinges schulde do seruice, So þat oure lorde Ihesu criste espouse [20] te þe soule be take aboue al þinges : for as moche þat þe soule may be þer fed & refestid of þe comfortabel wordis of his espouse.

10   Þe sustris first wole be confessid whan it nediþ & schul resseyue twies eche moniþ in reuerence & deuocioun þe ful holi bodi of owre lorde Ihesu criste, & also ȝif it likiþ hem eche sonday in lentyn & in þe Auent, but ȝif it so be þat ani of hem bi resonable cause leeue hit & bi licence of þe Abbesse.

15   THe sustris & þey whoche seruyn Schal fast fro þe fest of seint Fraunces [21] til þe fest of þe resurrexioun of oure lorde, And from þe Assencioun of owre lorde vnto Pentecoste, Forasmoche þat þey [Fol. 55ᵛ] may plentiuowseliche | resseyue þe grace of þe holi gost, owte take þe sonday onliche & þe fest of alle Halwyn [22] & Cristmas day & þe 20 fest of sent Stephin & Seint Iohn euangelist & þe Circumsicioun & Epiphanye & þe purificacioun. But from þe resurrexioun of oure lorde till þe Ascencioun & fram Pentecost til þe Fest of seint Fraunceyse þey be nat boundin to fast, but þe Fridayes & oþer fastis whoche been ordeynid & bowndyn generali bi holi chirche. 25 And þey may sureli drinke wyne & ete fisshe & eyrin & chese & soche oþer þinges as perteyniþ to mylke. And also fro þe Natiuite of oure lorde til septuagesme þey may, ȝif þey wole, to-dite here metis wiþ grece owtake Friday & saterday. Also fram þe Fest of alle halwyn [Fol. 56ʳ] til the Fest of þe Natiuite of oure lorde & in lentoun & in | Fridayes 30 and in fastingdayes whoche been generalli I-stablid bi holi chirche, þe Sustres schul nat ete Eyrin ne cheese, ne none oþer þinge þat perteyniþ to Milke, but in all oþer times þey may use hit. The sustres beinge in gode hele & þey þat seruin kepin hem alle dayes fram etinge of flesche. And also þey whoche been hole in bodi 35 schul faste eche Friday wiþowte fische, but ȝif it falle so þat þe Abbesse dispense wiþ hem, as it is acustumyd, ȝif any Fest solempne

* MS. '& þat', superfluous.

come on a Friday . This maner of Fastinge & of abstinence forseyde, þe ȝonge sustris wiþ inne þe age of xv ȝere be nat boundin to kepe, ne þe ouer agid, ne þe fiebel, ne þe sike, to þe whiche after her febelnesse þe Abbesse may merciabli purueye comunliche alle dayes, & in oþer þinges necessaries | to þe sustris. And to hem whoche seruyn, [Fol. 56ᵛ] & to þe ȝonge sustris wiþ inne xviii ȝere þe Abbes may dispense in fastinge after þat it schal like to here goodli, saue in aduent, & in lentoun & in friday & in fastinge dayes whiche been enstablid bi holi chirche. The sustris whoche been lete blode been nat boundin to fastinge in þe time duringe bi þre dayes, safe in lentoun & in 10 fridayes & in time of advent, And in þe time bitwene þe Ascencioun & pentecoste, & þe fastinges whiche been enstablid bi holi chirche generali.

And also þe Abbesse muste be ware þat sche suffer nat þe sustris to be lete blood ouer iii times [23] bi þe ȝere, but ȝif it be for 15 certayne cause enspecial & necessarie. And algatis þat þey be nat lete blode of any seculere persone straungere, | & nameli of [Fol. 57ʳ] a man by none resoun, ȝif it may be as goodli.

Of þe syke sustris whan sykenesse falliþ bi grete cure & diligence, as ferforþe þat men schul mowe or se for to do, þat þey been seruid 20 bi alle maner þinges in metis & drinkes whoche been gode for þoo maladies, And in alle oþer þinges nedeful be wey of charite feruent benyneli, couenabelliche & ententifeliche. And þey whiche been sike schullin haue proper place in þe whiche þey schul dwelle desseuerid from hem whoche been in helþe of bodi, For as mochel 25 þat þe reste & þe ordinaunce of [þe] Couent be nat distourbid be none wey.

The abbesse, for as mochel þat sche schulde be a clere myroure & ensaumple to alle þe sustris, þat sche enstrengþe her as mochel as sche | may for to suen continueli þe couent & þe comune life. The [Fol. 57ᵛ] abbesse þat wole nat ne may nat lede þe comune life, be assigned [24] wiþowte tariynge of þe office for to gouerne oþer bi þe mynster or bi þe visitouris of þe ordre, [bot] ȝif it so be þat þe Abbey had none harme, bi cause of here longe dwellinge in þe office or ellis þat mani grete & schewynge profites þere of comme *. 33

Silence, be it of alle Sustres holden in soche maner, þat þey speke nat wiþoute licence ne one to oþer, ne to none oþer, sauynge þe

* MS. 'comune'.

88 *The Rewle of Sustris Menouresses enclosid*

febel & þe syke. But alle gates þat þe Abbesse, or presedente
take kepe ententifeliche in whoche place, whan, & howe sche schal
gif licence to sustris for to speke. And þat alle sostres enstrengþe
hem to vse signis religious & honestis. At dowble festis & at
[Fol. 58ʳ] Festis | of apostles, & any oþer dayes after þat it schal best like to
þe Abbesse, * from þe howre of none til euynsonge or ani howre
couenable, The sustris may speke of oure lorde Ihesu criste & of þe
solempnite of þe Feste present & of good ensaumplis of seyntis &
of oþer þingis honeste of whoche þey haue for to speke.

10 Whan anybodi to any of þe Sustres schal speke, First schal þe
Abbesse be warnid þer of or þe president, & ȝif sche graunt, þanne
schal þe suster speke wiþ þe straunger so þat sche haue two oþer
sustris at þe leste wiþ here, þat þey mow see & here what þat þey
doo or speke, boþe on þat one syde & on þat oþer. And allegatis
15 þat þe sustris whiche haue for to speke to any straunger, þat þey
[Fol. 58ᵛ] be welware þat þey aboundyn nat hem | for to speke in vayne wiþ
owtyn profite & houre longe.

Neuerþeles whan any of þe Sustris wole confesse her, bi þe perloure make her confessioun in privite alone to one. The confessoures,
20 þe whoche schullin be assingnid bi þe Minster general or bi þe
prouincial, assoyle hem of alle sinnis. None of hem schal speke bi
þe grate of yryn bi þe whiche þey schullin be huslid & here diuine
office & sermones, but be auenture þat it be for cause resonable &
necessarie & wiþ compani, after þat it is ordeynid & establid to
25 speke ; & algatis þat it be seeldyn. This grate[25] of yren be hangin
wiþin a blacke cloþe, so þat bi resoun none suster may be seyne þer
þorw & þat none bodi may see none þinge wiþ inne, but ȝif it so
[Fol. 59ʳ] be for a resonabel cause, þat þe same cloþe | be drawyn agayne bi
licence of þe Abbes ; & in þe same maner schal be holden a blacke
30 cloþe at þe perlour whiche some may be done awey bi licence of
þe Abbes & of þe Assentement of grete parti of þe couent; &
þis gratis schullyn haue doris of yren bund & naylid whoche schal
be alwey closid but ȝif it be for þe causes forseyde.

Þe perlour be of many & þicke roddis of yren, of stronge werke
35 forgid. Þis perloure to confessioun schulle be made in þe Chyrche,
oþer in oþer place couenabel after hit schal beste seme to þe
mynster, & þat þe gratis be of mani & thicke roddis of yrin bisili
forgid & of stronge werke. Allegatis in one of þe sydis of þe

---

* MS. adds 'And'.

The Rewle of Sustris Menouresses enclosid 89

forseyde grate be a smalle wyndow I-made wiþ a goget of yrin, bi þe whiche þe preest, whan he schal heue vp his honde, may mynistre to þe Sustris goddis bodi, and þat none bodi may putte his honde wiþinne þe grate be ani partie of þe grate. And þe forseyde [Fol. 59ᵛ] goget alwey schal be closid wiþ two keyis, in þe warde of a persone 5 couenabel & honeste, sauing whan þe sustris schullin resseyue goddis bodi & here sermonis, or bi oþer cause resonable after þe Iugement of þe Abbes. Wiþowte licens of þe Ministre þer schal nat be in þe couent but one whele couenable, bi þe which we takiþ to þe sustris þat whiche schal * nede to hem & take awey þat 10 whiche is nedeful; & þat þis whele be made & ordeynid in soche wise þat none þinge may be seyne bi þat. Bi þis whele schal none Suster speke to nobodi, but two whiche kepin þis whele wiþ grete diligence.

And also like as þe abbesse beriþ here, make sche alle þe sustris for to kepe be hem alle bisili | þe ordinaunce of silence of þis present [Fol. 60ʳ] rule. † For as mochel þat alle materis to speke wiþ inne be forbarrid in alle þingis to alle sustris, sauinge þat þe Abbesse may speke to here sustris at houris & in places couenablis as it schal be moste plesaunt to god. The sustris sike in þe time of here maladi in þe fermeri, & þey whiche been seruauntis, & oþer hole sustris bi 20 cause for to visite þe sike charitabli bi licence of þe Abbesse entringe in to þe fermeri, may speke wiþ sike sustris after disposicioun of þe Abbesse.

MOreouer we comawnde estreyteli in vertu of obedience, þat none Abbesse ne ani suster suffer nat ani persone,²⁶ what euer he 25 be, for to entre wiþoute especial licence of | þe apostle wiþinne þe [Fol. 60ᵛ] Abbey or cloyster, ne wiþ inne none place where þat þe sustris been abidinge, be he religious or seculere or of what maner dignite. And also we defendin þe entre to alle maner folke, excepte þe kynge²⁷ in whoche Reine þis Abbey is foundin, whoche kynge may 30 entre to hem wiþ þe numbre of x personis, & excepte þe Minister general of þat ordre of Freris Menoures, wiþ ii honest felowis, And excepte þo whiche of þe comaundement of the Abbesse & bi counsayle & assentement of þe moste wise suster schal enter inne to hem for a grete nede wel schewinge of ani werke nedeful or mater 35 profitable; þe whiche, ȝif þer be many, þan þat þer be many

* MS. adds 'nat'.   † MS. repeats 'for as mochel': crossed through.

suffisauntli ordeynid þe same werke to performe. And whan þat |
[Fol. 61ʳ] werke is doon, þat wiþoute tariynge þey been made go oute of þe
place; & in soche materes & causis þat þe assentement of þe Ministre
prouincial be requirid whan it may be done couenabli, for as moche
5 þat þe clerete of here renouns be sauid & kepte. The mynistre prouincial of þe same prouince may entre into þe Abbey wiþ ii honest
felawis bi cause necessari for to visite & refourme þe couent. And
also in oþer materis & causes whoche happin for to come, þat may
nat be reformid wiþoute entre amongis hem, þe forseyde Ministre
10 prouincial schal entre, if* þat þe Ministre general bi counsayle of
most wise sustris þer schal to hem graunt. ʒif it happe bi auenture
þat any Cardinal wole come & entre in þe Abbey, þat he be res-
[Fol. 61ᵛ] seyuid in reuerence & deuocioun, but | þat he bringe nomoo saue x
persones. Anoþer prelate,[28] to whom is grauntid any time bi þe
15 apostle for to entre wiþ inne þe Abbey for to blesse þe Abbesse or
for to sacre a sustre, or in any oþer maner þat it be grauntid at any
time to any Bischop for to singe masse wiþ inne, it schal suffice for
to haue wiþ him iii or iiii personis to ministre duli to him. And
whan it schal be grauntid to any man wiþ inne þe gate for to
20 abide, þe Abbesse may speke wiþ him alle dayes, wiþ ii of moste
demures & wise sustris of þe couent. ʒif it happe any time þat any
womman haue licence to entre in to þe Abbey, þe sustres may speke
to here bi conge of þe Abbesse. & Allegatis þat þe sustris take gode
kepe þat wiþ alle diligens þey eschiewyn þat none of hem at here
[Fol. 62ʳ] knowynge speke to noman þat | is entrid, but in þe maner & bi
ordinauns forseyde, sauinge to vertuous men & to honest, whoche
been here confessoures, or to oþer in here stede, & þat in couenable
time to here † consolacioun & edificacioun of here sowlis, some times
þey may speke bi licens of þe Ministre generale or prouincial or of
30 þe Abbes, so ii or iii Sustris be þere present to herin & to see. Of
þis same maner be take kepe, þat þey whoche haue graunt to enter
inne in þe Abbey been so honeste of spekynge & of here maneris
& of her life & of here abit, þat þe sustres whoche seen hem may
vertuousli be edified in here sowlis & none mater of disclawnder
35 þer of for to rise. Alle þoo whiche bi licence of þe apostle wole enter
wiþ inne, First þey schullen to þe Abbesse & to oþer wise sustres
[Fol. 62ᵛ] of þe couent | schew here letres of þe apostle of here graunt.
Whan any of þe sustris been greuou[s]li syke, þat sche may nat

* MS. af.   † MS. repeats 'here' superfluous.

godeli come to þe perloure for to be confessid or for to resseyue
goddes bodi or oþer sacramentis of holi chirche, þan here confessoure arayid in vestimentis longynge to a preest excepte þe
chesiple schal entre wiþinne, & his felaw reuestrid alle in white;
þat þan þe sike suster confesse here bi soche maner þat iii oþer 5
sustris be so nyʒe þat þey may se þe same confessoure & also her
whoche is confessid. And whan þe confessioun schal be herde or
any oþer sacrament ministrid, like as þey come inne reuestrid, so
goo þey owte, ne dwelle þey þer inne, ne wiþ any oþer Suster speke
þey nat, but in þe forseyde maner. And also | whan any comendacioun [Fol. 63ʳ]
schal be done for sowlis of Sustris, or for obsequies of any of hem
dede, ii freris menoures or preestis preuoyres or þre, whan þe bodi
is brought to entierment, schalle mowe entre reuestrid wiþ ornementis longynge to a preest, and þey for to do alle þat longiþ to a
preest in soche cas. And be þey alle wey to gyderes bi alle þe time 15
þat þey schullin be ocupied abowte þe execucioun of þe same office,
and þat fulfillid for to departe þennis wiþowte tariynge. And also
þat gode kepe be takyn of the Ministris, & bi him whoche schal be
visitoure in þat tyme of hem whoche schal entre in to þe Abbey for
any soche werkis to make ʒif þey be necessari, whan & how þey 20
schullin entre, & gouerne & haue hem wiþinne. And up þat þey
ordeyne and dis|posin þer of as hem schal best like, so allegatis þat [Fol. 63ᵛ]
þe name & þe gode fame of þe Sustris be sauid in alle poyntis.

For to kepe þe forseyde entre duringe þe tyme, one of þe sustris
best louynge god, wise & vertuouse, be ordeynid & enstablid & in alle 25
maner of diligence þat þe keyes of þe same entre be saueli kepte &
putte in saue warde of þe forseyde sustre keper in þat case assignid,
so þat none dore ne gate þer be nat openid wiþoute verray knowinge
of þe same Suster. The oþer keye alle diuers schal þe Abbesse kepe.
And also þat þer be assignid & ordeynid an oþer suster for to be 30
felow & helpinge to þe forseyde porteresse in alle times & in alle
þinges longinge to þe same kepinge, whan þe chief porteresse schal
be ocupiid oþer weyes re|sonabeli in þe nedis of þe Abbey necessari. [Fol. 64ʳ]
And ful ententli þat þis porteresse suffer nat þat þe dore be nat
openid but whan þat grete nede askiþ it, & þat þe dore diligentli 35
be kepte & schet & þe Guyches of barris of yrin & þe openinge be
nat any tyme lefte wiþoute warde of one of þe forseyde porteresse,
& þat it be schette be day & be niht wiþ ii keyes, & þat it be nat
openid to sone at eche knockynge, but ʒif hit so be þat þe porteresse

firste see bi þe smalle wyndow who þat he is, & þat it is none
dowte but þat he þat knockiþ be soche a persone whoche may
lefolli come inne after þe rule of þe same religioun aforseyde. We
wole of alle þinge, þat þe ȝate be of hihenesse þat þer may nat come
[Fol. 64ᵛ] þer to but wiþ a ladder,²⁹ whoche be lefte | vp & vnder a chayne of
yrin, & schet wiþ a keye; & in þe mornyninge whan it is day, bi
þe chayne avale bifore iii of þe sustris. We graunt that þey haue
a lowe ȝate, where þorwe þat þey may bringe Inne grete þinges as
tunnys of wyne & oþer þinges like, & þat it be schette wiþ locke &
10 keye & diligentli I-kepte . And ȝif it hap any tyme þat any werke
be for to do wiþ inne þe Abbey, & þat seculeris persones muste
enter þere for þat, þan þe Abbesse puruoye & ordeyne iii sustris
wise, sad, & vertuouses of þe Couent, whiche kepe hem in silence to
alle þo persones whiche schal make werke, & algates þat none oþer
15 persones entre. And ȝif it happe þat þer be multitude & prees, þat
[Fol. 65ʳ] oþer persones honest & couenable be ordeynid & chaun|gid³⁰ for to
helpe þe forseyde sustris to kepe þe same ȝate sureli & bysili.

OF þe visitacioun of þis religioun : be alle weyes ordeynid þat who
þat schal¹be establid Generall or special visitoure, þat he be soche
20 one whoche is wel knowen of stedfastnesse of religious life & gode
vertuis; þe whoche whan he comiþ to þe Abbey & is entrid wiþ
inne, þat he bere him & schewe him soo þat he may drawe þe
Sustris from goode in to beter, & þat he enstrengþe hem in þe loue
of oure lorde, & þat he alwey estabel amonges hem feruent desire in
25 charite. And whan he schal entre bi reson [*of visitacioun* *], þat he
take him ii religious felawes honest & couenable, þe whoche felawes,
[Fol. 65ᵛ] wille þey be wiþinne þe Cloyster, schulle nat departe | asunder by
none time. Alle þe Abbeyes of þe same religioun been I-visitid eche
ȝeer ones or at þe leste in ii ȝere ones. The visitoures be algatis of
30 þe ordre of Freris menoures & þat he be I-sent by þe minister general
of the ordre.

AT alle ȝeres þat þe Abbey may nat be visitid bi þe visitoure,
whoche ys sent fro þe mynister generale, ȝif it be nedeful, þat þan
þe abbey be visitid bi þe Mynister of þe same prouince after þe

* Words supplied by comparison with Latin original.

The Rewle of Sustris Menouresses enclosid 93

forme of þe Rule of þis religioun forseyde . The visitoure whiche wole goo ferþer in his visitacioun,[31] after tyme þat þe rule ys redde, enquere he besili þe trowþe of alle Sustris & of eche of hem bi hemselfe generali, & especiali þe estate of alle þe sustres & how þey kepin here religioun ; & þere he fyndiþ any defawte, | for to amende [Fol. 66ʳ] & refourme hit in þe principal & in þe membris in jelosie of charite & in þe loue of rihtwisnesse & bi grete discresioun in alle times.

WHan þat he visitiþ[32] in alle times any of þe Sustres, þe Abbesse schal abide oute of þe chapitre, & *resigne þe seele, & sche schal nat be at here owne visitacioun ; & none þinge be purposid of one suster to anoþer, but þat whoche may be prouid haue be done by comune spekynge or bi apert knowynge. An ouer alle þinges[33] þat he take kepe & þenke bisili & nameli in þe visitasioun of þe Sustres, þat stere nat to any þinge but to þe loue of god for to speke of, & of þe amendement of þe Sustris whoche wole nat knowe here trespace & þe defauhtes whoche been putte on hem, ȝif | þey [Fol. 66ᵛ] wole excuse hem of þe same ; & ȝif it be grete þinges, audience schal nat be denyed to hem. And þoo sustris whoche acusiþ oþer of greuousis þinges, ȝif þey faylen in prouing þer of, after þe blame whoche is put vppon hem, be lawfullich punischid. And þe trespace or defaute whiche haþ be punischid biforne bi a visitour, schal [*nat*] be redressid of newe. The visitoures schullin kepe þe maner of spekynge forseyde, þat is for to vnderstonde, þat þey speke to alle þe sustris or to ii at þe leste bifore mani whiche be nat ferre ; & also whan he is oute of þe place & wole speke to one or to many of þinges whiche perteyniþ to his office.

And we wole þat þe visitoures spede hem of here visitacioun of alle wiþ owte greuauns | of þe Abbey, & algatis þat wiþinne iiii dayes or [Fol. 67ʳ] v atte moste bi here visitacioun, but ȝif it so be þat it nediþ lenger to abide for hope & grete nede. And after þat þey for to haue none power to entre in to þe Abbey. The time of þe visitacioun whoche is aboue seyde schal nat be esloignid wiþowte special conge of þe Mynistre. And we wole nat þat þe generalle Minister dwelle ne

* MS. adds ' þe '.

abide lenger but þe same time, but ȝif it so be for a grete certayne
cause. Allegatis at þe nyhte from þe sonne goynge to reste til in
þe morwe at þe sunne risinge, þat none be suffrid for to dwelle or
to entre wiþ inne, neyþer visitour ne oþer, of what auctorite þat he
be * warnid, but ȝif it so be þat it be for confessioun for to here of
[Fol. 67ᵛ] any | sike Suster gretli syke or for any grete peril schewynge. And
wolyn & monestyn ententifeli, þat þe Sustres in priue & aperte
þo þinges whiche after þe forme, as it semiþ to doo to kepe here
rule, whoche been to establid & to amende, After þat whoche schal
best seme to hem & þer vppon þat þey myngin & preposin couenabli
& besili to visitoure to whom þey been holden by vertu of obedience
for to obeye stedfastli wiþ in þe time forseyde In alle þinge
longinge to þe visitoures office. And ȝif þer be any Suster þat haþ
trespassid aȝenst þe Rule, be sche punyschid rihtfulli bi þe visitoure,
as it longiþ for to be done. The abbesse also, ȝif here meritis & here
defawtes axen hit, be sche assoylid of here office bi þe visitoure &
[Fol. 68ʳ] bi him also corec|tid. The couent & oþer familieres, ȝif þey be re-
prouable in any þinge, þat þey be repreuid; & ȝif þey wole nat be
repreuid, þat þey be algatis remuyd. The confessoures & here
felowes be of þe ordre of freris Menoures, whoche þey schullyn
dwellin þere & minister þe sacrament of þe awter & oþer sacramentis,
but ȝif it so be þat Ministres general or prouincial ordeyne in oþer
maner bi cause resonable & honest. And ȝif þe visitoure fynde any
cause notable ageynist þese confessoures, he is holdin to enforme þer
of þe Ministre prouincial, whoche schal redresse hem or putte hem
awey owte of þe place.

AFter þat we enmonestyn straytli þe visitoure, þat þoo þinges
[Fol. 68ᵛ] whoche he fynt in his visitacioun þat | he kepe priue, ne schewe hit
nat bi his knowinge to none bodi, but assone as misdedis schal be
redde & penaunce enioynid, alle þat whoche is writen schal be brent
bifore þe couent, but ȝif þer be soche þinges whoche bi þe counsayle
of moste wise sustris of þe couent schul be reportid to þe Ministre
general of þe ordre. And also ȝif so be þat þe Minister prouincial
finde after þe visitacioun any þinge notable ageynis þe visitoure or
ageynis his felawes, He is holdin to make enformacioun to þe Minister

* MS. repeats 'that he be'.

general. The felaws to þe visitoure schul nat be at þe visitacioun, but ȝif it so be þat þat it seme to þe visitoure for þe beste to doo.

The eleccioun of þe Abbesse perteyniþ alle oneli to þe couent, but þe confirmacioun quassacioun & deposing | perteniþ to þe Ministre [Fol. 69ʳ] general of þe ordre of Freris Menoures, ȝif he be present in þe prouince; & ȝif he be nat, þat it schal pertien to þe Minister prouincial, In þe whiche þe forseyde Abbey is foundid, To whom perteniþ þe ordinaunce of þis ordre, þe gouernaunce, þe cure, þe visitacioun, þe correccioun, & reformacioun, & bi hem & bi oþer visitouris after þat at it be enioynid hem in place & in time; bi þe whiche visitoures þe abbesse schal be assoylid of here office, as it is expressid aboue. And þere for þan in vertu of obedience we comaunde straytli senden & enioynen alle Abbessis & Sustris of þis religioun, þat þey be obedientis to þe Minister general of þe ordre of frere Menoures & to þe Minister prouincial of þe same prouince, in þe whiche þe same | Abbey is sette, in þinges whiche been nat ageynis [Fol. 69ᵛ] here sowlis, ne ageynis þis present rule. For we wole þat þey be alwey sogettis to here gouernouris. Also we enioynin to alle þe sustris of þis same religion, þat þey obey diligentli to here Abbesse, after þat þe Abbesse be confermid, as longe as þat sche dwelliþ & abidiþ in here office. Whan for maladi or for any oþer caas þat þe Abbey be destitute or voyde of an Abbesse, þat þan þe sustris schal * chesyn a president to whom in þe mene time þey schul be obedientis til a nyew Abbesse be confermid & ocupie here office. And þis same president schal vse & execute in þe mene time þe office who ys longynge to þe Abbesse.³⁶ The mynistris [and†] þe visitoures³⁶ schul refourme alle dis|honeste & amende alle þingis whoche been for to [Fol. 70ʳ] amende booþ in spiritualite & in temporalite. And it [is] for to eschiewen comynges & goinges of straungeris bi occasioun of temporal þinges & forasmoche þat þe Sustris may lyue more in pees for to serue god allegatis, þat þey haue in comune & for to resseyue þe profites of rentis & possessions & sureli to kepe. And for to trete þe forseyde possessions in riht maner, haue þey in þe forseyde Abbey a procuratoure³⁷ wise & trew, whoche schal be establid of the counsayle of the Abbesse & bi consentement of þe couent & be

---

* Before 'chesyn' a word erased, probably 'mow'. † MS. whoche.

he put owte at alle time, whan hem schal seme goode & profitabel;
& þat þe procuratoure be holdin to ȝeelde acounte resonable to þe
[Fol. 70ᵛ] Abbesse & to þe wise Sustres enspeciali bi þe couent þer|to assignid,
& to þe visitouris whan þey wolen herin of alle þinges whoche haue
5 be deliurid to him & þat he haþ despendid. And þis procuratoure
schal nat in none maner selle, ne bynde ne draw awey any goodes
or catallis of þe Abbey, & alle þat which is done in damage to þe
Abbey bi soche maner of bad gouernaunce, we Juge it for nawt & of
none auayle. And for as moche þat in oþer place is oure life
10 perpetuel, we wole aboue alle þinges þat þe sustris of þis religioun
eschuen outrage & þe sourfait of bigginge & of alle maner curiosite,
whiche been contrarious to alle godenesse & whoche god hatiþ in
alle þinges.

[Fol. 71ʳ] The seel of þe couent be kepte after þe ordinaunce of þe same
couent. And alle þe letres whiche | schul be sent from þe couent
schal be firste I-redde in þe chapitre. None of þe Sustres sende ne
resseyue any letres but soche whoche þe Abbesse schal rede first, or
ellis þat þe same letres be I-redde bifore þe Abbesse be anoþer suster
þer to assignid. The Abbesse schal holde chapitre eche wike twies
20 at þe leste, one of coreccioun & amonisschment, & anoþer of þe ordinaunce of Sustris. And ouer alle þinge we defende þat none
Ministre ne visitoure bi here auctorite make none constitucionis in
þe Abbey ageynis þe forme & rule aforseyde, wher þorwe þe sustris
be bounde or enclinid to any vice or payne, but ȝif so be þat it be
25 done bi consentment of alle þe couent; and ȝif ani soche nyew
ordinaunce be made, by no maner þat þe sustres schul be boundyn
þer to.[38]

[Fol. 71ᵛ] We seyn þan þat none persone of holi chirche ne seculer take in
despite ne varie ne transpose þis present rule correctid & approuid,
30 ne any þinges whoch been comprehendid þer inne, ne for to go
folili þer ageynis. And ȝif any be so hardi þat dare take þat vppon
him, knowe he þat he renniþ in þe wraþ of god almyhti & indignacioun
of þe apostles Peter & poule. This was ȝouin at vienȝ [39] þe vi
kalendis of august þe secunde ȝer of oure dignite.

The Rewle of Sustris Menouresses enclosid

This [40] is rule of sustris enclosid, whoche haue lefte alle þinges of þis worlde for loue of god. Certis þey do grete vnderstondinge, for in þis worlde may no man dwelle in profitabel pees. At alle dayes þer been enemyes And þerfor þat þe sustres put here þowtes for to loue god ententifely, whoche schal putte hem in goode place. And | for as mcchel þat þey been enclosid, allemihti god schal ȝeue [Fol. 72ʳ] to hem of his fayre þinges & þat is fayre paradise, bi cause þat þey haue louid him in vertuouse seruise. Now prey we þis gode ladies þat þey preyen for oure sowles þat we may come & haue þe Joye of heuyn bi his blessid grace perpetuelly for to endure. Amen.

Here endiþ þe Rewle of Sustris Menouresses enclosid

FOr as moche þat it is couenabel lowli seruauntes & deuowtes hand maydenes of owre lorde Ihesu criste for his loue þe worlde wiþ alle vaniteis to forsake, And þe batayle for to vndertake agaynes þe deuel & him for to wiþstonde & his temptacions, & hem [Fol. 72ᵛ] selfe to refreyne bi name of professioun, | bi whoche þey been submittid to diuerses obseruauncis of religioun, so þat þey mowen bi þe forseyde avowe of regulere obseruaunce helþe in sowle & bodi haue in þis worlde, And after here departinge for to reioyse perpetualli þe rewarde of blisse, whoche ys ordeynid for here rewarde, we perfor 10 fader spirituel of his þingis þenkinge wiþ gode diligence, hauin ordeynid þat þe sustris whoche been or schal been vnder þe gouer-naunce in þe cure of freris Menowres, alle þow þat þey be clepid Menowressis or of þe ordre of Seint Clere or of seynt damian[1],* or of what oþer name þat þey hauyn or berin, þat in eche place wher 15 þey been dwellinge bi þe ministris prouincial of þe Freris Menours [Fol. 73ʳ] & bi þe Abbesse of þe same place & of þe | couent or of þe gretter parti of þe couent be þer ordeynid be oure auctorite certeyne nombre of hem after þe quantite & sufficiant of godes & rentis longinge to þe same Abbey, so þat þey may of here goodes couenabli be sus-20 taynid.[2] And ouer þat certayne nombre bi þis maner assigned, þat none be resseyuid in þe same hous wiþowte special licence of þe apostle, But ȝif so be þat here godes & rentis been of soche encrese whoche may suffice to moo; & algatis byfore any soche resseyuinge, þat þe encrese of here godes bi þe grace of god be 25 denounsid to þe chapitre general of freres Menoures. Atte whiche chapitre it schal be þan ordeynid how many persones may þer putte inne ouer the nombre of olde time, bi resoun of þe encrees of here [Fol. 73ᵛ] goodes & reue|nuys, as it is forseyde. And ȝif it happe bi þe grace of god any persone or many persones for to be resseyuid ouer þe 30 olde numbre, Algatis þat none soche resseyte be made wiþ owte licence of þe Ministre general or prouincial, to þe whoche Ministris we comaundin straytli þat bifore ani soche graunt schal be done, þat þey auise wel, þat none couenaunt † þer in be made vnduli, ne

---

* The numbers given in the text refer to the notes which will be found on pp. 120-3.

† MS. 'comenaunt'.

The Rewle of Sustris Menouresses enclosid 99

ani þinge þat towchiþ Simoni. And ȝif it happe bi auenture þat
any of þe kynrede or oþer Frendes make legacioun, deuise or ȝifte
of ani maner possessioun, gode, catelles or Iuyelles to any Suster, þat
it schal be resseyuid bi þe Abbesse & dispendid in profite to Couent;
& sche bi cause of whom þat gifte is done for, þat allegatis sche 5
in here necessitees be holpyn & rele|uyd to here ese goodli. And [Fol. 74ʳ]
þat þe ministris be wel ware, boþe general & prouincial, þat for
none leue bifore grauntid ne after, bi none wey, for none coloure ne
requeste, ne for any oþer occasioun, none maner suster of þis religioun
bi here selfe ne be any oþer do resseyue or take any þinge whoche 10
is longynge to ani frere or to any Couent or to þe chirches or werkis
of þe forseyde ordre. And also þat bi resoun of soche resseyte none
þinge be procurid ne ȝouin, & þat none þinge be suffrid to be
resseyuid bi resoun of custume, ne bi any oþer wey, For alle soche
dedis we reccoune* corrupcioun. And ȝif any ministre do or suffer þe 15
contrarie, be he cursid in so mochel þat he may nat be assoylid ᵃ
but onli of þe pope † excepte peryl of deeþ, & ȝif he be conuic|tid [Fol. 74ᵛ]
þer of, þat þan he schal be deposid of þe office of Ministre perpetueli.

And more ouer we ordeyne þat þe Abbessis & alle oþer whiche
þe goodes of þe Abbey schal gader, resseyue, ministre, or despende, 20
eche ȝere þat þey schal ȝeelde acounte bifore þe Ministre general or
prouincial & before ani wyse Sustres I-chosin þere bi þe Couent, of
alle maner resseytis & expensis & of alle oþer þinges in diew maner,
& of alle þat whiche is owynge bi any persone, & of þe astate of þe
Abbey. And we wole also þat in eche hous of þe ordre in þe 25
biginnynge of þe Abbes, after þat sche is in pesible possessioun of
þe godes, & alle þinges whoche longyn to þe hous, þat wiþ inne
ii monþis in þe present of þe Ministre general or prouincial or | of [Fol. 75ʳ]
þe visitoure of þe house, & in presens of vi wise Sustris of þe same
place be an Inuentari made of alle here godes & catallis meuabel & 30
not meuabel; & þis Inuentari schal be regestrid or dowblid in alle
poyntis acordinge & enselid wiþ þe seeles of þe Abbesse & of þe
couent; and amongis oþer þinges in þe forseyde register be con-
teynid what bestis þey hauyn, & what þey been worþe, & what
corne þey hauyn, & what wynes, & alle oþer maner store, & þe 35
dettis whoche þe hous owiþ, & þe dettis whoche been owynge to þe
house, & to whom þey been bowndyn & þe names of here dettoures,
& what ornementis, & what vessel & couertoures, & what oþer

* MS. 'rettoune'.   † Word rubbed out, but still legible.

soche thingis been in þe hous. And ȝif any Abbesse resseyue þe hous in | gode estate & sche dooþ enpeyre hit, bi alienacioun or destruccioun of here godes or bi dette & foli obligacioun, þan be sche deposid of here astate, & ouer þat be sche punyschid as it longiþ
5 to. And we wole þat þe forseyde Inuentaries or regestris been redde opunli & playnli in þe Chapitre bifore alle þe Couent; and after tyme þat þey been redde, one register dwelle wiþ þe Abbesse, & þat oþer wiþ þe Couent, & þe transcrite wiþ þe Ministre general or prouincial.

10 And ȝit as we recordin oure blessid predecessoures pope boneface þe VIII *,[4] þat after a constitucioun bi hem ordeynid vppon þis same religioun, vnder vertuouse rule, þat alle þe Sustris schulden dwelle & abide vnder stedefast & perpetuel closinge, & as we been efformid In some placis of þe ordre | þis poynt is nat kepte holi, And þerfor
15 owre wille is, þat þis same constitucioun be kepte outerli. Wherfor we comawnde straytli to alle Ministris & Abbessis & to alle þo to whom soche kepinge of closure perteniþ, þat þey alle doo here feruent diligence for to kepe truli, þat none Suster priuyli ne apertli passe nat oute bi none maner wey, But ȝif so be in case þat
20 any of hem been sent & ordeynid for to edifie & ocupie a newe place of þe same religioun, or ellis þat it happe þat ani of hem be in so stronge maladie opunli, þat sche may nat dwelle ne abide þer inne wiþ owte grete sclaunder or perille importabel.

And ouer þat we wole þat none religious ne seculere, of what astate or dignite þat he be, þat he enter nat to hem | wiþowte licence of þe Apostle, owtake þes persones to whom is grauntid conge, bi here rule & bi ordinaunce of owre predecessouris . And ouer þat we comaundyn streytli to þe Ministris, Custodis & wardeynis bi þis tenoure present, þat þey distreyne alle here freris to
30 hem sogettis, þat in here comynges & abidinges in þe Abbey þey gouerne hem vertuousli in alle poyntis after þe rule of seynt Fraunceys & statu[t]es of holi popis † & oþer holi † Freris of þe same ordre. And alle þoo whiche doo þe contrari schullin be punischid & chastisid after þe ordinaunce in þe same statutes
35 assignyd.

And also sauynge in þe same rule of þe Sustris made bi seynt

* The word 'pope' is rubbed out and a line drawn through 'boneʿace þe VIII' in MS.

† Words have been rubbed out, but are readable.

The Rewle of Sustris Menouresses enclosid

Clare is a clause conteynyd, þat in eche house þer may be resseyuyd certay|nis personis for to serue hem & þe whiche schal be con- [Fol. 77ʳ] streynid to alle maner obseruaunces of professioun like as oþer been wiþ inne, owtake closure, &c., we neforþat, for þe honeste & gode fame of þe Sustris of þe ordre of seynt Clare or Menoressis or of seynt Damyan, Oþer weyes we ordeyne at þis time, & wolin þat oure ordinaunce endure perpetuelli, whiche is þis þat we comaundin straytli þat from þis time forþe, soche seruauntis þat now been or schullin been, þat þey been as ferforþ & astraytli boundin to þe obseruaunce of profess:oun as oþer sustryn in þe same Abbey vnder obedience, & þat þey dwellin & abide perpetueli vnder closure. Neforþan þey schul mowe haue in eche house of soche religioun certaines wommen | but fewe, þe whiche schullen be of gode age & wel auysid & of [Fol. 77ᵛ] goode maneris & honestes in seculere habite; & soche schal entre nat in þe closure of þe Sustres, but for profite of þe Abbey & for grete necessite to þe Sustres, after þat is enioynid to hem, & þat þey be þere of warnid. And ȝif þe Abbesse take vppon here ageynes oure comaundement for to goo owte of þe forseyde closure, or geue licence to any of þe Sustris, þat þan bi þe Ministre in þe counsayle of þe freris, The same Abbesse schal be remewid of here gouernaunce, & þe Sustris bi þe maner goynge owte of þe closure, but in case sufferablis, schullyn be made onables to alle offices of þe ordre, & neuerþelese þat þey been enioynid to do þe penaunce assignyd & ordeynid in þe ordre | for greuouses trespasis. [Fol. 78ʳ]

And also we defenden straytli þat þe Sustris of þe order, haue none cellis in here dortoure, & ȝif any þer be, we senden & comaunden þat bi þe ministris or be visitoures in þe nexte visitacioun þat þey do destruye vtterli alle soche maner cellis; & ȝif any oþer be counsaylinge procuringe or helpinge þere agaynes, þat þey been chastised & punischid sadli by censure & sentence of holi chirche & that by oure auctorite. And ȝif any of þe forseyde Ministris or oþer freris of þe same ordre presumyn now or in tyme comynge to make oþer statutis or obseruaunces ageynes owre ordinaunce forseyde, we bi auctorite papal* enioynyn & comaundyn þat soche constitucions been holden for nauhte & of none valu. And we wolen | & comaunden [Fol. 78ᵛ] straytly þat alle þe Ministris prouinciallis in alle here prouinces do sende to alle Abbeyes of þe same ordre whoche been or schulde been vnder cure & goueinaunce of freris Menoures, The copies of

* Word rubbed out, but readable.

5

10

15

20

25

30

þis ordinaunce enselid vnder þe sele of þe mynistre & of þe diuynitoures, And þat þey been redde to þe sustris in here couentis opynli & þat þe Ministris comaunden stray[*t*]li þat þis ordinaunce from þis time forþe be I-kepte entierli & holdin stedefastli wiþ owte any
5 variaunce or lettinge.

At alle þe houres þey schal first a litel ringe & make a suffisaunt restinge, so þat þe Sustres may make hem redi & assemble in þe chirche wiþ owte tariynge, & þan schal þe belle be rungyn wel [Fol. 79ʳ] lenger, & þis maner ringinge be vsid in alle times, safe | in dobel
10 Festis[5]. For þan we schal ringe iii tymes longe boþe to euensonge & to matynnis, bi espacis suffisauntis. And at þe tierce twey tymes longe with couenabel espace, & after þe tierce iiii time to þe masse couenabli. Eche day we schal ringe in time longe bifore þe biginninge of þe Inuitatorie[6]. On sundayes, at dobel Festis, &
15 semydobel þey schal ringe, whan þe[*y*] byginne *Te deum l[audamus]* tille soche a verse *pleni sunt celi & terra*. And on sundayes whan þey syngen þe ix respons[7], while *Gloria patri* is asinginge, þan þey schal ringe til þe biginnynge ageyne of þe response. Whan þey been at þe leuacioun[8], þey schal ringe a litel in þe masse
20 conuentuel withowte more. At þe mete & at þe soper in alle times [Fol. 79ᵛ] þey schal sowne þe smale belle, And after | til þe Sustren haue wasschin here hondis & assembel togyderes bifore þe freytoure, & after here refeccioun þey schalle smyht iiii strokes on þe belle of þe freytoure. And after þis smytinge þe Sustres schullin rise
25 & entre honestli in to þe Freytoure, & after þat þey schal sowne þe belle, bi þe space of seyinge of iiii *Aue maries*. And after þat þe Chauntresse in sesynge of þe sowninge schal seye *Benedicite*[9]. And þe Couent schal answere in þe same tune. And þan þe Chauntresse schal bigynne þe verse, & alle þe couent schal sey after.
30 At *Iube d[omne]*[10] Sche þat schal rede fromme þe ende of þe Couent til sche come in myddis of þe Couent schal sey *Iube d[omne]* & bowynge schal resseyue þe blessynge. And in þe end of þe mete, þe refrey- [Fol. 80ʳ] touresse schal smyte | iiii strokes on þe smale belle, & anone þe reder schal sey *Tu autem*[11]. And þe Sustres at þe tabel schul seye *Deo*
35 *gratias*. And after anone þe Somenerere schal sowne þe smale belle as longe til þe sustres been fro table, & in renges bifore, one

The Rewle of Sustris Menouresses enclosid 103

Suster ageynis anoþer. And þan þe chaunterere schal biginne þe
verse & alle þe couent after, & atte *Gloria patri* Eche Suster schal
turne ageynis oþer. Whan alle is done, þe almoynere schal turne
here towarde þe ymage[12] & sey *Agimus tibi*[13] wiþ *Benedictus deus
in do[nis]*, And after þat þe Chaunterere schal bigynne for to go to þe 5
Mynystre wiþ *Miserere mei, deus*, & alle þe couent & þan þe quere
on þat one syde schal take his verse, & þe Quere on þat oþer syde
schal take anoþer verse. And assone as þey | haue bowid hem to þe [Fol. 80ᵛ]
ymage reuerentli, þey schul go in to þe chirche singyng þe same note.
And at þe entre of þe Quere þey schul bowe towarde þe awter, & 10
whan þey been entrid in here segis þey schul stonde one ageynes
anoþer, til þey sey *Retribuere*[14]. And þanne alle schal bowen at
Per dominum, & þanne turne hem te þe auter til me seyþ * *Fidelium
anime*[15]. And whan þey haue answerid *Amen*, þey schul bowe
& sey *Pater noster*, ȝif it be Fest, stondinge; ȝif hit be Feri, 15
knelinge; And after in þe ende smyte þe forme & seye *Deus det
nobis s[uam] p[acem]* and þe couent answeringe *Amen*.

WHan þey ȝelden graces at þe soper in þe Freytoure, þey schul
do as it is seyde biforne, saue þat þey schullyn nat knele but bowe &
seye | *Deus det nobis s[uam] p[acem]* wiþ owte smitynge, & answere, [Fol. 81ʳ]
Amen. And þey schul honestli in silence goo owte of þe freytoure,
sauinge þoo whoche þey schul seruyn.

And also at þe colacioun[16] whoche schal be done eche day in þe
freytoure, First þey schul sown þe belle in Monastre bi espace
auenaunt, & refectuouere schal sowne þe smale belle of þe Cloyster 25
be as longe time þat alle þe Sustris may be redili ensemblid in þe
Freytoure. And anone after þe Redere schal sey *Iube domne, &c.*,
& resseyue blessinge bowinge, as hit is forseyde. The benisoun is
þis: *Noctem quietam & finem perfectum concedat nobis omnipotens
& misericors dominus*. ℞ *Amen*. And after þe firste or secunde 30
verse of þe lessoun þe Reder schal sey *Benedicite* wiþ | titel & poynt- [Fol. 81ᵛ]
ing in tone of a lessoun. Þe blessing is *Potum ancillarum suarum,
&c. In nomine patri[s] & filii & s[piritus] s[ancti]*. ℞ *Amen*. And in
þe ende of þe lessoun þe Reder schal sey *Fratres, sobrii estote &c. . Tu
autem d[omine] &c.* ℞ *Deo gratias*. The sustris schul goo to monastre 35
ordeyneli seyinge, *Miserere mei, deus* wiþ owte note, & þan þey schul

---

* 'me' and the þ of 'seyþ' erased and 'þey sey' in later hand in margin.

104 *The Rewle of Sustris Menouresses enclosid*

ringe þe grete belle in þe clogere for complin, whan it is ronge & seyd in þe chirche *Adiutorium &c.* & *Pater noster* knelinge. Þan þey schal sey *Confiteor &c.* & *Misereatur &c.* And as oftyn þat fastynge day is, Collacioun schal be done & seyde & nomore. And
5 in oþer tyme þey schal come to Complyn as to oþer houres of þe day. And þe time þat þey schul slepe bi day Fro Pasche vnto
[Fol. 82ʳ] seint Croyse. . Sche þat haþ redde at þe tabel, as sone as sche haþ etin, sche schal sowne þe smale belle of þe freytour bi þe space of an *Aue maria.* And after anone þe Sustris schullin rest hem in
10 pees & silence & in þe time of slepinge none persone schal be wiþ in þe cloos but þe sustris oneli.

Whan þey schullin goo in to chapiter, þey schul sowne þe smale belle longeli, & anone wiþ owte tariinge þe Sustres schal assemble in þe Chapitre ; & whan þe Sustris been ensemblid at þe Monastre
15 & þat þe last stroke is smetyn, þe ebdomodari[17] make a tokin in smytinge þe forme wiþ here honde honestli, & anone þe sustris schul bowyn hem ȝif it be a Fest ; but if it be a feri, knelinge & seyinge *Pater noster.* And after þat þe ebdomo[da]ri make a syngne,
[Fol. 82ᵛ] as | hit is aboue seyde, for to make hem redi & þan sche schal
20 bigynne þe office in here sege & here visage turnid to þe awter. And so schal alle þe sustris do til *Gloria patri.* And þan schal þe one syde of þe Quere turne hem ageynis þe oþer in obeyinge. Alle in þis maner schal þey be whan þey seyn þes psalmes wiþ owte note in þe Quere. Alle sustres schul stonde vpriht saue in þe
25 psalmodiinge at þe seruice of dede, for þan þey schul sitte. Whan II psalmis or IIII been seyde vpon one antime[18], þe quere schal stande vp while þe antym ys bigonne excepte at prime & in tyme of Pasche & at Complin. In alle oþer times boþe one & oþer schul stonden & sitte chaungeabli sauing at *Laudate d[ominum] o[mnes]*
[Fol. 83ʳ] *g[entes], & laudate d[ominum] de celis,* | *Quicunque uult, Benedictus, Nunc dimittis, & Magnificat,* Wher þey schullen alwey stonde, wheþer þey rede or singe, & an oþer time, at þe office of oure ladi, whan it is seyde wiþ owte note. But at þe lessons whan þey schul sey psalmodi, þan þey schul sey distinctly & atrete, & also whan
35 þey haue seyde & endid on þe one syde þe verse til time þat þe oþer syde schal biginne þe oþer verse, & specialli in þe offices of oure ladi & of þe dede. Whan þey synge, þat þey make none treyne ne poynt of metre, but þat þey make pause euenli & auenauntli. For to ȝeue þe antemes & for to tune þe psalmis

The Rewle of Sustris Menouresses enclosid

þer schul be ii chaunteressis, one in þat one syde & one in þat oþer
side in eche quere ordeynid & assignid, whiche schullen | ȝeuin þe [Fol. 83ᵛ]
antemis & entune þe psalmis eche on here syde, & þe chauntresse
whiche schal ȝeue þe anteme schal entune þe psalmes. And
a anteme schal neuer be bigonne of tweyne bifore þe psalme. Þe 5
lessonis schullen be redde in myddes of þe quere ; þe responses boþ
bi day & bi nihte schul be songoun sittinge in here seges, like as
antemis been. Whan þat * *Iube d[omne]* riht in middis of þe quere,
sche schal obey to þe awter for to resseyue þe benysoun, & þe
Ebdomodari schal sey þe benisons sittinge, after time þat sche is 10
sette. But þe benisons of þe Gospellis sche schal euer sey booþ bi
day & be nihte & nat chaunge here voyse, but in one poynt, &
nameli benisones chaungin neuer for festis ne for feri. The absolu-
cions[19], as *Exaudi, domine, Ipsius pie|tas & A uinculis*, alle wey [Fol. 84ʳ]
schullen be seyde in here places & in dayes ferialis þe one after þe 15
oþer, alle þowe þat a Gospel be seyde. The benisons[20] been *Euan-
gelica leccio &c*, & þe oþer II schul alle wey be seyde whan þe
Gospel is seyde, be it fest, be it feri. The absolucions schullin be
seyde in þe tune of chapitres, þe benisons in þe tune of lessons.
And also þe orisouns at þe houres of þe day, of prime, of mydday, 20
& of none, schul be determinyd vnder þe tune of chapiteris ; & þe
Ebdomodari whiche schal sey þe orisoun schal sey *Domine exaudi
& Benedicamus domino* in þe same tune, & þey schul answere
Deo gratias, holdinge vppe. And þe orisons whiche schullen be
seyde at euynsonge & atte matyns þey schul be seyde vnder þe 25
same tune as orisons | at masse solempli. And in þe tyme of entre- [Fol. 84ᵛ]
dite general[21] þe Sustrin schul sey alle maner offices distinctly &
sympli wiþ owte note. Whan þe orisoun is seyde in ferial day, hit
schal be seyde knelinge til *per dominum* & so schal þe orisons of
owre ladi & of seynt Frauncesse, but þe orisoun after *preciosa* schal 30
be seyde at alle tymis like as þe *Pater noster* schal be seyde. At
þe bigynninge of houres, & in þe ende whan þe *pater noster* ys
seyde booþ bifore lessons, & at þe blessinge of þe tabel, & whan
graces schul be seyde in þe Freytour, þey schul nat knelin, & at
þe *preces* of prime & of complyn & at þe suffragis of euensonge & 35
matynnis, whoche been seyde in lowe & þe orisons[22] whiche been
songoun schul be songoun (schal be seyde) stondinge ; & whan þe
preface[23] is seyde at masse, þey | schul knelyn at þe orisoun til [Fol. 85ʳ]
Dominus uobiscum, be it Feest or feri, & nat biforne & so for to

* Some words must be supplied here, e.g. 'sche seyþ'.

106 *The Rewle of Sustris Menouresses enclosid*

stonde til *Per dominum*. And also after þat þe Offertorie [24] is
songoun til *orate, fratres*, þe sustres schul turne hem riht towarde þe
awter. And [*whan*] *Orate* is seyde, þey schul knelin til *Per omnia*,
& þanne rise vppe & bowe hem towarde þe awter til *Sanctus*, & þan
5 þe one syde of þe Quere agaynes þe oþer & singe *Sanctus*, & after
þat for to knelin duringe þe leuacioun of þe bodi of oure lorde Ihesu
criste, & þan rise & worschip deuowtli on knees towarde þe awter,
& þey schul dwelle greuelinge [25] til *Per omnia* at *Pax domini*.
And whan *Agnus dei* is seyde, [þey] schal lye greueninge til þe
10 Post com[*munions*].[26] And in festiuale dayes & Festis of ix lessons
[Fol. 85ᵛ] & in masses of *Requiem* whoche been songyn in soche Festis, | þey
schul nat make prosternacioun whan *Sanctus* is in seyinge, til þe
leuacioun, but after þe leuacioun þey schul make prosternacion til
Per omnia of þe *Pater noster*. And of masse of *Requiem* for bodi
15 present, of whom vigilies were done bi note in a Ferial day, þey
schal do as in a festival day & so schul þey doo at masse of þe holi
goste, of oure ladi, of seint Fraunces, and in massis for anniuersa-
riis, & of oþer seintis; & in þis massis of seyntis þey schal sey
Kyrie, Sanctus & agnus, as of Festival dayes, þow it be feri. Item
20 þey schul knelin in ferial dayes at *Salue, sancta parens*, & at *Veni
sancte spiritus*, & in þe massis of þe holi goste & of oure ladi, & in
lentyn at þe verse of þe tracte,[27] *Adiuua nos deus salutaris noster*
[Fol. 86ʳ] & at *Salue regina* & *Aue regina*, & at þe bigyn|ninge of þe verse
O crux, aue, spes unica &c. And in eche time & place þat þey
25 knelin in ferial dayes, þey schul knelyn in festival dayes, except at
preces[28] of prime & of complyn. And also þat þe sustris been riht
turnid eche agaynis oþer. In þe masse whan þe Offertori is
songoun, þey schulle turne hem towarde þe awter, & after þe *Sanctus*
also þat þey been vpriht, & at alle times þat any is songe in
30 comune. Item alle times þat *Gloria patri* is seyde, þey schul bowe
hem lowli, & at *Te deum laudamus*, whan *Te ergo quaesumus* is
seyde, & at *Credo* whan *Homo factus est*, & at *Gloria in excelsis*,
whan *suscipe deprecacionem* is seyde,& in þe endis of ympnis, & whan
þe last verse saue one of *Benedicite*[29] is seyde. Item þe benisoun
[Fol 86ᵛ] after complin | schal be seyde bifore þe anteme & after þe anteme
þey schul sey *Fidelium*. Item *Te deum & Credo* schal be songoun,
as it was ordeynid at þe chapitre general. Item þey may singe som
sequence [30] bi ordinaunce general, as þe ordinal makiþ mencioun
except at þe masse of holi goste.

In lentoun þey schul sey þe Intrat *Dum sanctificatus nos fuero* * Item þe antemes *Lux orta est iusto* And to oþer soche lyke instede of *In eternum* For *alleluia*, whan one *Alleluia* ys seyde . And also *Rex gloriose* & soche like may be songin some time for a Fest solempne in þe note of *Eterna lux.* Oþer ymnys 5 schullin be songe in alle times after þe ordinal, whoche schal nat be chaungid for Auent ne for any Fest ne for lentoun. Item þey schul nat leuyn for masse of þe holi gost, or of oure ladi, ne for | any [Fol. 87ʳ] oþer masse, but for þe masse of þe ordinari schal be songe in his place & at þe riht houre. Inuitatoriis & alle oþer verses & 10 *benedicite* schul be seyde in alle times of one Suster in here sege in Festis of ix lessons & of iii lessoun, & ʒif it be dubbil fest or half dobel, ii Sustris schul sey þe verse bifor þe awter. And in feriis bitwix paske & pentecoste, *Alleluia* in þe masse schal be seyde alwey wiþ ıı Sustres . And in festis of ıx l[e]c[ions] & in sondayes, 15 Inuitatori & þe last Respons & *Alleluia* in þe masse schal alle wey be songe of ıı sustris at þe lectroun in myddes of þe Quere. In Festis half dowble þe orison alwey schal be seyde in myddis of þe Quere at þe first euynsonge & at þe secunde & at þe matyns & in þe ııı & vı | Respons & at þe grayel of þe masse & of ıı sustris & [Fol. 87ᵛ] þe smale verset, but ʒif þe chapitre at þe secunde euynsonge be chaungid. For a feste simple þan be it done as þey may godeli, & ʒif it may be atte euynsonge & at matyns þat þer be had an cierge or a chaundel of wexe & especialli in half dowbel festis & on sondayes. Þese been þe half dobel Festis.[31] Seint lucy, seint 25 Nicholas, þe fest of Innocentis, of seint Thomas of Caunterbiri, þe vtas of þe Epiphanie, þe fest of seint Anneys, & of seint Agase, þe fest of þe holicrosse, þe apparicioun of michel, þe octaues of þe ascencioun & of seint Antony, & of seynt John Baptist, þe fest of seint Marie magdalene, þe translacioun of seynt thomas, & þe fest 30 of seynt | Margare, þe vtas of seint laurence, & of seynt lowis, & þe [Fol. 88ʳ] fest of þe decollacioun of seint Iohn, þe vtas of þe Natiuite of oure ladi, the fest of seint Martin, þe fest of seynt Elizabeþ, & of seynt Cecile, & of seynt katerin, & þe vtas of corporis cristi.

In festis douce dobles,[32] þe Abbes or sche whiche schal do þe 35 office in þe ende of þe thrid stroke, boþ of þe one euynsonge & of þe oþer [33] & of Matyns, schal go to þe lectroun in myddis of þe Quere . And þere ıı sustris ʒongest apparaylid schullen holde eche of hem a cierge in here honde, þe one in þe riht syde, & þe

* So the MS. : it should be *Dum sanctificatus fuero in vobis.*

oþer in þe lefte syde, & þe þrid schal holde a censer ful of fyre ;
& as sone þat sche schal see a tokene made for to bigynne þe office,
[Fol. 88ᵛ] þat sche turne here bifore here whoche schal bigynne | þe office &
anone encense III times bifor þat þe signe be made, þan turne here
5 towarde þe awter, And þe Quere þe one syde agaynes þe oþer,
whan þe Pater noster is seyde. Þan anoþer tyme schal þe signe
be made & alle þe sustris schul ryse up & stonde riht towarde þe
awter at *Deus in adiutorium* & singe also, and whan þey come to
Gloria patri, alle schul bowe, þe one Quere agaynes þe other. Whan
10 þey come to *Sicut erat*, sche whoche biganne þe office returne here
to here sege, & þan þe cierges schullyn be I-sette bifore þe awter
ordeynli. The chaunteresses schul stonde in middis of þe quere &
bygynne to gyder alle þat longiþ to here office. Sche whoche doþ
þe Office schal biginne alle þe antemes of *Magnificat & benedictus*
[Fol. 89ʳ] & þe | *Inuitatori & Benedictus* schal be seyd of IIII, & þe bigyn-
ninges of þe Respons of matyns & alle þe smale Responses at alle
þe houres schullen be seyde of II in myddes of þe quere bifore þe
auter. Whan þey ensence in þe quere, ȝif it be a dowbel fest, þey
schul first ensence here whoche dooþ þe office, And after þe chaun-
20 teresse in myddes of þe quere, & þan þey schal ensence eche syde
of þe quere, & þan þey schul ensence þe ceroferessis II * times or
IIII times at þe moste. In þis maner þey schul ȝeue þe pees.
Whan it is dowbel Feste or encense, þey schul biginne towarde þe
semennere & þerfor to gyffe of þe pees. Whan þey schal sey þe
25 orisoun, hit be seyde in myddis of þe Quere. Sche whoche dooþ þe
office & oþer wiþ cierges schullin be vpriht as longe þat þe orison
[Fol. 89ᵛ] is aseyinge. & þe ebdomodarie schal | goo to here seege & sey þere
Fidelium.

This been þe Festis doubles.³⁴ Noel, Fest of seynt Stephen, seynt
30 Iohn, þe Circumsicioun, þe Epiphanie, þe fest of conuersioun of seynt
poule, þe purificacioun, & alle þe festis of oure ladi, þe fest of seynt
antoun, & his translacioun, *Cathedra sancti petri*, þe Fest of seint
Mathee, of seynt Gregori, of seynt Benet, Pasch wiþ II dayes after,
þe Fest of seynt Marke, þe fest of þe ascencioun, & of Pentecoste
35 wiþ II dayes after, & of þe blessid Trinite, & of Corpus cristi, &

* MS. 'IIII times or II times at þe moste'.

The Rewle of Sustris Menouresses enclosid 109

þe Fest of seint Fraunces, & þe vtas of seynt barnabe, & seynt
Iohn Baptiste, of seint Petir & Paule, & þe commemoracioun of seynt
paule, þe vtas of seynt Petir & seynt paule, of seynt Iames, &
ad uincula sancti petri *, of seynt laurence, of seint Clare, & þe
vtas of owre ladi, & þe fest of seint lowis bisschop, of seint [Fol. 90ʳ]
barth[olem]u, of augustyn doctor, of seint Matheu, of seint Misshel,
of seint Ierome, of seint luke, of seynt symon & seynt Iude, þe
Fest of alle halwyn, þe translacioun of seynt lowis, þe fest of dedi-
cacioun, & of seynt andrew. In alle þese festis þey schal haue IIII
ciergis at masse, at euinsonge, & at matyns, II at þe auter & II 10
at þe chandelabris. In alle oþer times þey schal haue II ciergis.
At masse, whan þat þey syngin in þe quere, Comunly þe one syde
of þe quere schal turne hem to þe oþer side, but at þe chapitres
towarde þe awter, & at þe orisons whan þey bowen hem or makyn
prostracioun & whan þe offertori is seyde, þey schul turne hem 15
towarde þe awter til *Sanctus*, whan þey encline hem or make
prostracioun. At orisoun, be it at masse or | houres, þey schul [Fol. 90ᵛ]
stonde vp whan *Per dominum* ys in seyinge & turne towarde þe
auter til *amen* ys seyde. Whan one suster seyþ þe Inuitatori or
biginniþ an anteme or seyþ a schort Response or *Benedictus*, sche 20
schal turne here to þe awter, and one [*syde*] of þe Quere ageynis
þe oþer. Whan þey sey *Flectamus ge[nua], leuate*, þey schullin
turne hem to þe auter after *leuate* til þe ende of þe orisoun. At alle
þe orisons þey schal do so, saue at þat whan þey seyþ *Dominus
uobiscum*, at þe whiche þey schal knelin til *Per dominum*. At 25
alle þe orisons of þe masse & of houres þey schul turne to þe awter,
& at þe orisoun after *Asperges*.³⁵

Item whan masse of þe feri ys seyde in a Festiual day, alle
maner obseruauns schal be kept as in a feri. Item whan þe office
of owre ladi is seyde, þey schal | haue a cierge or a chaundel ʒif it [Fol. 91ʳ]
may be. Item in þe ende of alle þe houres þey schul sey *Fidelium
anime &c. & pater noster*, ʒif þere schal nat be bigune a masse or
a houre anone after, & to make a signe wiþ prosternacioun & sey
dominus det n[obis] s[uam] p[acem], but ʒif it be after Complyn
or after matyns, & þe sustris schul answere *Amen*. Whan þey sey 35
many houres to gederis³⁶ wiþ in þe couent or owte, þey schal sey
Fidelium after eche houre & *pater noster*, & anone after bygynne
anoþer houre. Whan þey haþe I-smyten þe forme for to encline or

* MS. 'scē petre'.

for to rise vp, þey schul sey *Fidelium anime &c.* & whan þey haue seyde þe *pater noster*, þey schal seye *Dominus det &c.*

In festis [*of*] ix l[e]c[ions] ii Sustres schul sey *Alleluia* at þe lec-troun ʒif it be to sey; ʒif þe tracte be longe, hit may [*be*] songen [Fol. 91ᵛ] of iiii or of vi, þe one after | oþer. In festis half doubles & in sondayes ii sustris schul say þe Grayel & iiii *Alleluia* & mo ʒif it lyke for to do. Whan þey syngiþ *Alleluia* in Feriallis dayes at þe first tyme wiþ owte endynge of þe newme [37] after þe verse, be it songyn til þe ful ende of þe newme. And whan þey singiþ ii
10 *Alleluia*, as in tyme of pasche, from þe vtas of pasche til þe vtas of Pentecost, þey schal singe þe firste *Alleluia* alle & his verse & it schal nat be bygonne ageyne bifor his verse ne after. Þe secunde *Alleluia* schal be bigunne bifore þe verse & after.

THe sustres schul kepin hem from goynge & comynge custumabli
15 þorwe þe Quere but bicause of necessite grete.

The maner for to hoselin þe sustres in massis conuentuales: first
[Fol. 92ʳ] þey schul sey her *confiteor* in here | places knelinge lowliche, & whan þe preest haþ assoylid hem beinge in here places, Eche of hem wiþ lowe voys ones schal sey *Non sum digna &c.* And þan
20 anone ii sustris schulle be redi for to holdin a towayle bifore þe preest. And þe freris whoche schal hosel hem, schal first hosel þe ministressis of þe awter, & after þat hem of þe Quere ii & ii to gydris of þe syde of þe quere, ordeynli alle with deuocioun & knelinge & þan for to drinke of þe chalis, and after þat for to
25 returne in here places agayne.

AT þe blessinge of þe tabel [38] at mete, but whan þey haue propre, *Oculi omnium. Gloria patri. Sicut erat. Kyrieleison. Criste eleison. Kyrieleison. Pater noster* [℣]. *Et ne nos* [℟]. *Set libera nos*; & þan sey *Oremus* on hye wiþ *Benedic nos, d[omine]* & [Fol. 92ᵛ] [*hec tua*] *dona &c.*, Blessing | wiþ here honde opynli; answere *Amen*. And anone aftr þe listresse schal seye *Iube d[omne] benedicere*. Þe benisoun, *Mense celestis &c.* answere *Amen*. In þe ende of þe mete, after *Tu autem* & answere *Deo gratias*, þey schul sey [℣]

The Rewle of Sustris Menouresses enclosid 111

Confiteantur tibi &c. [℣] *Gloria patri. Sicut erat.* And sche whoche haþ blessid þe tabel schal turne here to þe ymage, ȝif any be in þe freytoure, & seyinge on hye, & syngynge *Agimus tibi gratias &c.* answer *Amen*, & after þat seyinge þe psalme *Miserere mei, deus* wiþ all þe versis[39], *Gloria patri, Sicut erat, Kyrieleison, criste eleison. Kyrieleison. pater noster.* [℣] *Et ne nos* wiþ alle þe versis & in þe ende [℣] *Sit nomen domini benedictum.* [℟] *Ex hoc nunc* & seyinge wiþ owte *oremus* [40] *Retribuere dignare &c.* [℟] *Amen.* [℣] *Benedicamus d[omino].* [℟] *Deo gratias.* [℣] *Fidelium anime per &c.* answere *Amen.* Atte soper | *Benedicite,* [Fol. 93ʳ] answere *Dominus.* [℣] *Edent pauperes &c. Gloria patri . Sicut erat . Kyrieleison Criste eleison. Kyrieleison*, as it is seyde aforne after *Tu a[utem]* & answere. *Deo gratias.* [℣] *Memoriam fecit . Gloria patri . Sicut erat .* and after þat *Benedictus &c.,* psalme *laudate dominum &c.;* & in alle times *laudate* schal be seyde atte soper.

Whan þey etiþ but ones on þe day, þey schul sey benisoun & graces as at soper wiþ þe psalme *Miserere mei deus*. This ordinaunce of þe Benysoun & of graces schal be kept in alle times excepte in festis whcche haþ propre.

The benisoun on Cristismasse day & bi þe vtas: *Benedicite &c.* [℣] *Verbum caro f[actum est], alleluia.* [℟] *Et habitauit in nobis, alleluia Gloria patri . Sicut erat;* & in þe ende after *Tu a[utem],* [℣] *Notum fecit d[ominus], alleluia.* [℟] *Salutare s[uum], alleluia. Gloria patri. Sicut erat.* On twelfeþe daye and bi þe vtas, *Benedicite.* [℟] *dominus.* [℣] *Reges | Tharsis & insule munera* [Fol. 93ᵛ] *of[ferent] &c.* [℟] *Reges ara[bum] &c , alleluia. Gloria patri &c.* At þe ende of þe mete [℣] *Omnes de saba &c., alleluia.* [℟] *Aurum & thus defer[entes], alleluia.* psalme *Deus iudicium.*

On schere þursday [41]*Absolute** wiþ owte note & wiþ more sey[i]nge at þe mete *Cristus factus est pro nobis o[bediens] usque ad mortem,*

* MS. '*Absoluimus*'.

& þan schal be seyde *Pater noster* lowli & wiþ owte ani more [42] blesse þe tabel, & wiþ [*owte*] *Iube d*[*omne*] & wiþ owte *Tu a*[*utem*]. And whan þe lessoun is redde & endid, & after þat þey haþ smetyn vppon þe tabel, as it is vsid at þe lessons of þe dede, þan þey schul
5 sey as biforne *cristus factus est &c.* psalme *Miserere* wiþ owte *Gloria patri*, but þe *Pater noster* alle lowe; & after wiþ owte seyinge *Oremus, Respice, quesumus domine &c.* & wiþ owte pronunsinge *Qui tecum & Fidelium*, but after þe orisoun þey schul seye *Pater noster* & nat sey *Dominus det nobis.*

[Fol. 94ʳ] In þis same maner graces schul be seyde on gode friday, sauynge þat þey schal ioyne to þe verse *cristus factus, mortem a*[*utem*] *crucis.* On pasche euyn. [℣] *Benedicite &c.* [℣] *Vespere autem sabbati, que lu*[*cescit*] *in prima sa*[*bbati*]*, alleluia*: *venit maria magdalene & altera maria vi*[*dere*] *se*[*pulcrum*]*, alleluia. Gloria*
15 *patri*, & in þe ende as bifore euynsonge, þe psalme *Laudate*, & þat may be seyde II times or more, til þey comyn to þe quere. On pasche day to þe soper in the saterday nexte, *Benedicite &c.* [℣] *Hec dies quam fecit dominus, alleluia.* [℞] *exsultemus & letemur in ea, alleluia . Gloria patri . Sicut erat &c.,* . After mete, *Hec dies.*
20 psalme *Confitemini.*

On ascencioun day & be alle þe vtas, [℣] *Ascendit deus in iubilacione, alleluia.* [℞] *Dominus in voce tube, alleluia. Gloria patri. Sicut erat &c.*; After mete [℣] *Ascendens cristus in altum*: [℞] *captiuam d*[*uxit*] *c*[*aptiuitatem*]*, alleluia . Gloria patri . Sicut erat*
25 *&c.* psalme *Omnes gentes.*

[Fol. 94ᵛ] On pentecost day & bi þe vtas. [℣] *Spiritus domini repleuit orbem terrarum, alleluia.* [℞] *Et hoc quod continet omnia, sci*[*entiam*] *habet vocis, alleluia. Gloria patri . Sicut erat &c.* After mete [℣] *Repleti sunt o*[*mnes*] *s*[*piritu*] *s*[*ancto*]*, alleluia.* [℞] *Et coe*[*perunt*]
30 *loqui, alleluia. Gloria patri . Sicut erat .* psalme *Magnus dominus &c.* And on þe Trinite sonday þey schul sey þe comune graces.

THe auent of oure lorde alwey schal bigynne on þe sonday bitwix þe v. kal. of December & þe III Nones of december, & also general rule þat þe IIII times namyd ymber dayis schul be holdin þe first
35 wednisday after þe Fest of seynt lucie & þe First sonday of clene lent & in pentecoste wike & after þe day of exaltacioun of þe holi Croys.

And also a general rule, ȝif any fest of any apostle or euangelist or of seynt michel | or of þe holi Croys, or any oþer fest whoche haþ proper respons, or any other fest generalli double fal on a sonday, þere as none estori [43] shal be first entrid, þe offise shal be seyde of þe fest, & memori of þe sonday at þe first & secunde euynsonge & at matyns & at masse ; & þe IX lessoun schal be of þe sonday. And whan a stori schulde be first entrid & may nat be I-putte ouer vnto anoþer sonday, þe fest so fallinge schal be deferrid til monday nexst after, & ȝif þe stori whoche shulde be songyn in þat same sonday be deferrid in to þe nexst sonday after, þan þe fest shal be songen in þat sonday wiþ a memori of þe sonday, except þe fest of alle halwyn. But oþer festes, whoche be nat doble, schul be deferrid til after, as it is forseyde. What maner festis of IX lessonis oþer þan | þe forseyde comyn on þe sonday schullyn be deferrid vnto monday, except þe fest of seynt Thomas Caunterbiri, & þe festis of seynt Siluester,[44] of seynt leon, & seynt Eustache ; & ȝif in þe same Monday be anoþer fest of IX lessons, hit schal be deferrid til tiewesday nexst after, & so schullin oþer festis be seruid þat fallyn on oþer dayes, til þey been seruid, But ȝif it be a Fest of apostel or Euangeliste or anoþer feste whoche haþ propre Respons or ani oþer fest double generalli. And soche simple festis of IX lessons whoche may nat be seruid for soche maner festis biforseyde been seruid on þe morwe after. Also festis solempnis in oþer londes & places schullyn be seruyd in þe same dayes whiche þey fallin on. For þe courte of Rome dooþ in þe same maner. Whan many festis | of IX lessons simple fallin continueli togyder eche fest after oþer, at þe secunde euynsonge of þe first feste, þey schalle chaunge þe chapitre of þe fest folwinge ; but ȝif* þe fest whoche comyþ after falliþ on oþer of whom þey makeþ solempne memorie, at þe first euynsonge after þe first orisoun, þer schal be seyde a memorie of þat same fest, & after þat a memorie of þe fest biforne. And þis is for to vnderstonde, þat festis simples or lasse be þo festis whoche be nat dowblis, ne of þe holi Croys, ne of þe awngelis, ne of þe apostlis, ne of þe Euangelistis, ne festis solempnis in some londis & some placis. Eche vtas þat is nat double is Iugid for a fest simple or lasse, excepte þe vtas of þe Epiphanie. Eche fest of IX lessons whiche is seruid on | Saterday, be it of þe apostlis or oþer, whoche be nat doubles

* MS. adds 'in'.

except þe fest of Innocentis, þey schul chaunge at þe chapitre of
þe sonday or of þe fest or of þe vtas; wherfor þat þe seruise of
sonday is lefte, & þey schul make memori of þe fest biforne, but
ȝif it be a dobel fest, þey schul make only memori of þe sonday.
And whan any fest is seruid on þe sonday, þey schal nat chaunge
at þe chapitre at þe secunde euinsonge, but ȝif it be soche a fest
on þe monday of whoche þe seruise schal be seyde on þe sonday, ȝif
it falle þer vppon. Of a fest þat is nat dowble whoche is seruid on
þe monday, at euynsonge of þe sonday þey schul make memorie
þer of wiþ owte more, ȝif it be nat a fest of apostle, or of euangeliste,
or anoþer fest whoche haþ propre Respons, | or a fest solempne
generali in some londis & in some placis; For soche maner of
festis, þey schal chaunge þe chapitre at euynsonge, & make memori
of þe sonday. At þe secunde euynsonges of festis dowblis of þe
holi Croys, of aungelis, of apostlis, of euangelistis, of festis solem-
pnis generali in some londes & in some places, þey schul make
memorie oneli of þe feste folwynge on þe morwe, ȝif it be nat a
fest double or anoþer feste whiche is equypollent, þat is for to
vnderstonde, a fest of þe same dignite, or þe vtas of a fest whan
þey chawngiþ at þe chapitre of þe fest folwinge; except þe festis
whoche hauen vtas, whoche Festis comyn wiþ in þe vtas of Noel,
þe whoche hauyn secunde euynsonges; except þe fest of translacioun|
of seynt Fraunceys,⁴⁵ of whom is made memorie whan it falliþ in
þe vigillis of assencioun, or Pentecost, but ȝif þe seyde Fest Translacioun of seynt Frauncesse come on þe morwe of Ascensioun, þan
memorie schal be seyde of þe translacioun of seynt Fraunceys, But
ȝif so be þat in som place þe chirche of þe freris be halwid in þe
name of seynt Fraunceys; For in soche places, & in soche chirchis
þe euynsonge schal be seyde of seynt Fraunceys & memorie of þe
Ascencioun. And it is for to know þat in þe vigil of a double fest,
þe euynsonge schal al be seyde of þe dobel fest, & ȝif in þe same
day be a fest nat dobel or sonday neyþer of þe one ne of þe oþer
schal be made memori except in lentyn & in aduent, for in þo
times memori schal be made of þe sonday. And it is for to knowe
þat at alle double Festis þe | antemys schullyn be doublid at euyn-
songe & matyns wiþ owte more. Also ȝif a fest of ix lessons come
wiþin any vtas wiþin which vtas þey seyn of þe Fest þat so fallin,
þe euynsonge schal be seyde fro þe chapitre forþe of þe Feste,
whiche so falliþ, but ȝif so be þat þe fest come on a monday or on

The Rewle of Sustris Menouresses enclosid 115

þe morwe whiche hath vtas; For þan þey schul sey on þe sonday
of þe vtas & memorie wiþ owte any of þe fest, ȝif it be nat a fest of
apostle or of Euangelist, or a fest whoche haþ propre Respons, or
fest solempne generali In some londis & placis. But at þe secunde
euynsonge of a lasse feste, þey schal sey fro þe chapitre forþe of 5
þe vtas wiþ memorie of þe fest. And ȝif þe fest come on a sonday,
hit schal be deferrid ȝif it haue none propre Respons, except þe
fest of seynt leon | pope, whoche schal nat be deferrid. And hit is [Fol. 98ᵛ]
for to vnderstonde þat in alle times þat wiþ inne any vtas, festis
been seruyd euermore at euynsonge & matyns, þe last memorie schal 10
be seyde of þe vtas. And hit is for to know þat wiþ inne vtaces alwey
þey schal sey at *Magnificat* þe antym of þe secunde euynsonge of
þe Fest. But at þe first euynsonge of þe vtas þey schal sey at
Magnificat þe anteme vppon *Magnificat* in þe vigil of þe feste.
Also ȝif a fest of III lessons come on þe daye folwinge after þe fest 15
of IX lessons, at þe secunde euynsonge of þe fest [*of*] IX lessons, þey
schul make memorie of þe fest of III lessons. But ȝif þer be none
fest on þe day whoche comyþ bifore þe day in whoche is þe fest of
III lessons, þey schal chaunge | at þe chapitre at euinsonge, like as [Fol. 99ʳ]
of a fest of IX lessons. The Inuitatori schal be songen feriali & 20
þe ympnis of þe fest at þe nocturne schullin be songyn wiþ his
note. The psalmis feriallis wiþ here antemes, þe versetis & alle
oþer þinges schul be seyde of þe festis as of a fest of IX lessons.
After None seyde þey schal riht nauht do, but like of festis of
commemoraciouns. Ȝif it happe a fest of IX lessons to be differrid to 25
a day of þe fest of III lessons, or þat a fest of III lessons come on
a sonday of þe fest of III lessons, memori onli schal be made at þe
first euinsonge & at matyns & at masse & at þe IX lessoun ȝif it
haue propre, & ȝif it haue none propre legende, þe IX lessoun schal
nat be of þe fest of III lessons. Also ȝif a fest of whom | þey [Fol. 99ᵛ]
makiþ onli a memori come on a sonday, of þe same feste schal be
made memorie in þe masse & at þe firste euynsonge & at matyns
in versicle & anteme & orisoun & in þe laste lesson, ȝif it haue
propre legende. And ȝif it so be þat in þat sonday, þey sey of
a fest of IX lessons & memorie made of þe sonday, þan þe last 35
lessoun schal be of þe Omeli of þe sonday, & þe propre legende of
þe feste of commemoracioun schal be lefte & þe memorie of þe sonday
schal be made bifore þe memori of þe feste of commemoracioun. Also
in festis whoche been seruyd in lentyn, alwey memori schal be

made of þe ferie at euynsonge & at matyns & þe last lessoun, ȝif it
haue an omeli. At þe festis whiche comyn in aduent, þey schal
do in þe same maner, except þe laste lessoun, ȝif þe fest come nat
[Fol. 100ʳ] in any | of þe ymber dayes. In none oþer tyme þey schal nat make
5 memorie of a ferie in þe day of a fest. Ȝif any fest haþ propre
stori & is nat entier, but is fulfillid of þe *comune sanctorum*,* þey
schal bygynne at þe secunde Respons. And generali alle times
þat þey make none þinge of properte of a fest, þey schul make
recours þe *comune sanctorum*. We make vtas of Noel, & III
10 dayes nexst after Epiphanye, of pasche, of Ascencioun, of Pentecoste, of seynt Antonye, of Corpus cristi, of Natiuite of seynt
Iohn Baptiste, of seynt peter & poule, of seynt laurence, of seynt
Clare, of þe Assumpcioun of owre ladi, of seynt lowis, of þe Natiuite
of owre ladi, & of seynt Frauncey̑s. Hit is for to vnderstonde
15 þat *Te deum laudamus* schal be seyde anone after þe laste lessoun
[Fol. 100ᵛ] fiom pasche | til þe vtas of pentecost, as wel in feriis as in festis,
& in alle times þat þey rediþ IX lessons, except þe sondayes fro þe
bigynnynge of auent til Noel & from septuagesme to pasche & in
day of Innocentis, ȝif it come nat on a sonday. And also it is for
20 to know þat whan þey rediþ nat IX lessons, þey schal rede III
lessons & singe III responsis, except from þe day of pasche til þe
Ascencioun & bi þe vtas of pentecoste & in þis þey singiþ II responsis,
alle þow þat III lessons be redde.

And also it is for to know þat *Gloria patri* is alwey seyde at þe
25 III respons, & at þe VI & at þe IX or last, except from þe sonday
of þe passioun til pasche But in þis time þey schal sey *Gloria patri*
in Festis whoche comyn þere, And in þe office [*of*] þe blessid virgin |
[Fol. 101ʳ] marie, owre swete ladi. And also it ys for to know þat in alle
festis þe antemis of þe laudes schullin be seyde at prime, at tierce,
30 at mydday, at none, bi order; But euermore þe IIII anteme is
lefte; & also þey schal sey hem at euynsonge, but ȝif þer be oþer
assignid. And it is for to know also þat in alle sondayis & alle
festis of IX lessons & of III lessons, þe orisoun whiche is seyde at þe
first euynsonge schal be seyde at alle oþer houris except at prime
35 & at complin & at euynsonges in lentyn, & in þe quater temps of
þe aduent whar þey singiþ þe grete antymes,[46] þat is to vnderstonde, *O sapiencia* & oþer.

𝕿his gode weike is ful complete blessid be þe holi Trinite, whiche
be his grace euer gouerne þis holi ordre in perfite charite. Amen.

* MS. adds '&.'

NOTES ON THE RULE OF SUSTRIS MENOURESSES

[1] *Urban.* This is Urban IV (James Pantélon, Patriarch of Jerusalem). Elected August 1261, died October 1264.

[2] *Alisaunder.* This is Alexander IV (Raynaldo, Cardinal Bishop of Ostia). Elected December 1254, died May 1261.

[3] *Kinge of Frauns.* This is S. Louis, otherwise known as Louis IX of France. He was brother of Bl. Isabella, who founded the monastery of Longchamp.

[4] *In owre monestre.* Latin 'in vestro Monasterio'.

[5] *And beene clepid bi þe name of sustris enclosid.* Latin 'cum Sororum inclusarum vocabulo nuncupandam concessit'.

[6] *And werevpon . . . meneres.* Latin 'Porro ex parte dicti Regis Nobis fuit humiliter supplicatum, ut dictam Regulam in aliquibus capitulis corrigi facientes nominationis ejus Minorum vocabulum adjicere de benignitate Apostolica dignaremur'. The later hand which has substituted 'þey' for 'we' has spoilt the sense.

[7] *Symon Deutre.* Latin 'Simonem tituli Sanctae Ceciliae Cardinalem'. This is Simon de Bria, afterwards Martin IV, elected February 1281. Died March 1285.

[8] *So that it was done as it was in name.* Latin 'ut sicut re, ita et nomine',

[9] *We ordeynid & establissin.* Latin 'duximus statuendum'.

[10] *But ȝif so be . . . forseyde.* The construction is here broken by misunderstanding of the Latin, 'Nisi de licentia, &c. . . . ad aliquem locum ejusdem Religionis aliquae transmittantur : quibus ad ipsum Monasterium, a quo transmissae fuerint, reverti liceat &c.'

[11] *Fole simplesse.* Latin 'fatua simplicitate'.

[12] *& also bi any . . . resonable.* Misunderstanding of Latin, 'nisi forte cum aliqua interdum causa valde rationabili exigente alicubi fuerit de consilio discretarum Sororum loci per praetactos Ministros, vel ipsorum aliquem dispensandum'.

[13] *To myne ladi seint Clare.* This is an addition peculiar to the English version and without anything to correspond to it in the Bull.

[14] *Of myne lorde þe apostle Boneface.* The Bull of Urban IV reads 'regulam a Domino Alexandro Papa IV Ordini nostro concessam, prout a Domino Urbano Papa IV est correcta, et approbata'. See also Introduction, p. 69–71.

[15] *þey schul be hosid & schod beringe none cordis & they schulle nat go alone.* Latin 'Soleas autem nunquam deferant, neque chordam'.

[16] *Ouereste cote.* Latin 'superiores tunicae'.

[17] *Whiche shal be made wiþ coriouste.* Latin 'nullatenus curiosam'.

[18] *From þe resurrexioun . . . ladi,* i. e. from Easter until September 8.

¹⁹ *xx Pater noster.* In Latin Bull XXIV.

²⁰ *So þat oure lorde . . . al þinges.* Latin 'cui [i. e. spirit of preyere] se debet Sponsa Christi mancipare'.

²¹ *Fest of seint Fraunces,* i. e. October 4.

²² *Fest of alle Halwyn,* i. e. Allhallows, November 1.

²³ *Ouer iii times bi þe ȝere.* Latin ' ne ultra quam sex vicibus'.

²⁴ *Be assigned . . . of þe ordre.* Latin 'sine morae dispendio a suo regimine per Ministrum, seu per Visitatores Ordinis absolvatur'.

²⁵ *This grate of yren . . . clothe.* The cloth hangs within the grating. Latin 'Hujusmodi siquidem cratibus ferreis niger pannus interius apponatur'.

²⁶ *Nat ani persone, what euer he be, for to entre.* In the early days of the Order, the Friars Minor were allowed to visit the Houses of Clarisses, but the Bull of *Quo elongati* published in 1230 forbade them to do so without a special licence from the Pope.

²⁷ *þe kynge in whoche Reine,* &c. Latin ' rege Franciae'.

²⁸ *Anoþer prelate,* &c. The translation has run two sentences into one. Alius autem Praelatus, cui forte aliquando intrare a Summo Pontifice sit concessum, duobus honestis sociis sit contentus. Quod si forte pro benedictione . . . alicui Episcopo concessum fuerit . . . tribus aut quatuor sociis sit contentus.'

²⁹ *A ladder, whoche . . . before iii of þe sustris.* Latin ' Porta . . . ad quam per scalam ligneam ascendatur, quae catena ferrea elevatur in sero; et cum clavibus firmetur et mane de die lucescente tribus praesentibus deponatur'.

³⁰ *Chaungid.* Possibly a mistake for ' chargid '.

³¹ *The visitoure whiche wole goo ferþer in his visitacioun.* Latin ' visitator ad visitationem procedens, &c.'

³² *Whan þat he visitiþ . . . seele.* Latin 'Cum autem visitatur aliqua soror, extra Capitulum commoretur. Similiter Abbatissa resignato sigillo, &c.'

³³ *An ouer alle þinges.* This passage is hopelessly corrupt. Latin 'Caveant autem Sorores et considerent diligenter praecipue in visitatione Sororum, ut nihil aliud, quam amor Divinus, et suarum Sororum correctio eas moveat ad loquendum. Illis autem, quae noluerint recognoscere culpam, quae ipsis impingitur, si excusare se voluerint, praesertim si gravia fuerint, audientia non negetur.'

³⁴ *And wolyn & monestyn.* Text corrupt. Latin ' Volumus et attente monemus, ut ea, quae secundum vitae suae formam et regularem observantiam statuenda fuerint, et emendanda, publice, ac privatim Sorores, sicut melius videbitur faciendum, Visitatori diligenter suggerant; cui per obedientiam teneantur in iis, quae ad officium suum pertinent, infra praetactum tempus firmiter obedire '.

³⁵ *þe office who ys longynge to þe Abbesse.* Latin ' quae ad Abbatissae officium pertinent '.

³⁶ *The mynistris and* [MS. whoche] *þe visitoures,* &c. Latin ' Minister autem et Visitator'. Note singular converted into plural in English version. The same occurs below (p. 96, l. 4) ' to þe visitouris '.

³⁷ *Procuratoure.* The procurators were first formally instituted by the Bull of Innocent IV of August 6, 1247, *Cum omnis.* (Sbar. i. 482.)

Ad haec liceat vobis in communi redditus et possessiones recipere et habere, ac ea libere retinere. Pro quibus possessionibus modo dicto pertractandis Procurator unus prudens pariter et fidelis in singulis Monasteriis vestri ordinis habeatur, quandocumque expedire videbitur, qui per visitatorem constitui et amoveri debeat, sicut viderit expedire.'

But, as Père Oliger points out, the Procurators can be shown to have existed at a much earlier date, even in connexion with S. Clare's House at San Damiano.

[38] Nothing in English to correspond to Latin: 'Volumus etiam et attente monemus, ne aliquid eis praecipiant, seu praecipiatur sine magna utilitate et valde evidenti et manifesta necessitate.'

[39] *Ʒouin at vienʒ.* Latin 'Urbem Veterem' (Orvieto).

[40] *This is rule . . . perpetuelly for to endure. Amen.* This paragraph is peculiar to the English version. There is nothing in the Latin Bull to correspond to it.

NOTES ON APPENDIX TO RULE

[The following Notes do not aim at commenting on or explaining the multitude of liturgical practices mentioned in this Appendix. Much of the material cannot be explained by separate notes. For example, the regulations as to the transference of Feasts cannot possibly be explained without setting out the Rubrics in the Roman Breviary, which deal fully with them. The author has made much use in these notes of Charles Walker's *Ritual*, '*The Reason Why*' (1908), and Addis and Arnold, *Catholic Directory* (1903); and he has received valuable assistance from the Rev. Dr. Francis Aveling.]

[1] *Seynt damian.* The Clarisses were frequently known as 'Damianites' or 'of Saint Damian', because the mother-house of the Order was that of San Damiano, where S. Clare was placed by S. Francis about a year after her profession and where she lived until her death in 1253.

[2] *So þat þey may of here goodes couenabli be sustaynid.* These regulations show a very marked departure from the ideals of S. Francis and S. Clare. Not only were the sisters to hold possessions, a thing quite repugnant to the principles which dominated S. Clare, but the number in any particular convent was to be determined having regard to the goods available for their support.

[3] *He may nat be assoylid but onli of þe pope excepte peryl of deþ.* For some offences it could be enacted that the guilty person could receive absolution from no one except the Pope, unless it were necessary to give him absolution when in imminent danger of death, lest he should die in mortal sin. Such are known as 'Reserved Cases'. The Bishops similarly have power of reserving cases so that absolution from them cannot be validly given by any ordinary confessor (Council of Trent, sess. xix, *De Poenit.* can. 11).

[4] *Oure blessid predecessoures pope boneface þe viii.* These words indicate that these constitutions were issued by some Pope later than Boniface VIII.

[5] *Dobel Festis.* Certain feasts are known as 'double' because the anthem sung at the Magnificat and Benedictus was 'doubled', i.e. sung throughout before as well as after the Canticles on the major festivals. Other feasts are known as 'semi-doubles', when half of the Antiphon was repeated before and the whole after the Psalm.

The above is the more modern explanation of the terms. An older explanation was that double feasts were so called because on them it was necessary to say the office of the Feast as well as that of the Feria.

[6] *Inuitatorie* is the Anthem of the Psalm 'Venite' (Ps. 94), chanted before, after, and interpolated with the verses of the Psalm: it is chanted at the beginning of Matins on all days except the Epiphany and the last three days of Holy Week.

[7] *þe ix respons*, i.e. the words said antiphonally after the ninth Lesson, when the Te Deum is not sung.

⁸ *þe leuacioun*, i. e. the elevation of the Host in the Mass.

⁹ *Benedicite*. This whole section will be readily understood only by comparing it with the Benedictio Mensae in the Roman Breviary. The main lines of the Benedictio Mensae are followed, with some slight variations of local custom.

¹⁰ *Iube domne*. It is doubtful whether the words in MS. should be transcribed as 'Iube domna' or 'Iube domne'. On the whole, the latter seems the more fitting as being the normal form. Moreover in one place [fol. 81ʳ] it is contracted 'dn̄e'.

¹¹ *Tu autem*. The versicle sung by the Lector at the end of the Lection at the close of the meal. In full it is 'Tu autem, Domine, miserere nobis'.

¹² *þe ymage*, i. e. the crucifix generally hung in the Refectory.

¹³ *& sey 'Agimus tibi' wiþ 'Benedictus deus in donis'*. Here two alternative forms are given: 'Agimus tibi, &c.' is said after Dinner (*Prandium*), and 'Benedictus Deus' after Supper (*Coena*).

¹⁴ *Retribuere*. The beginning word of the prayer: 'Retribuere dignare, Domine, omnibus nobis bona facientibus propter nomen tuum vitam aeternam'.

¹⁵ *Fidelium anime*. The end of the office of Benedictio Mensae: it proceeds 'per misericordiam Dei requiescant in pace'.

¹⁶ *And also at þe colacioun*. 'Collation' meant originally conference or edifying books read aloud in the Refectory after supper and before Compline. This is a practice required by the Benedictine Rule. Subsequently the word acquired a derived sense, viz. the light refreshment taken before the reading of the 'collations'. Addis and Arnold (*Cath. Direct.* 1903) refer to a statute of the congregation of Clugny (1308) where the word is used for this refreshment. In the present passage the office of Compline follows after 'collation' quite properly.

¹⁷ *þe ebdomodari*. These are the two sisters who for a week at a time lead the saying of the Hours in Choir.

¹⁸ *Antime*, i. e. Antiphon, a verse sung before the Psalm or Canticle, giving the key-note of it. In the Mass, the Introit, the Offertory, and the Communion are regarded as Antiphons.

¹⁹ *Absolucions*. These, each with its three appropriate 'Benedictions', will be found at the beginning of the Breviary. The first, 'Exaudi Domine', is used in the first Nocturn of an office of nine Lessons and on Mondays and Thursdays for offices of three Lessons. The second, 'Ipsius pietas', is used in the second Nocturn and on Tuesdays and Fridays. The third, 'A vinculis', is used in the third Nocturn and on Wednesdays and Saturdays. They are said before the Lessons.

²⁰ *Benisons*. In an office of three Lessons when a Homily is read with the Gospel, the first Benediction is 'Evangelica lectio', 'and þe oþer II' are 'Divinum auxilium' and 'Ad societatem'.

²¹ *Entredite general*. If the clergy of a country or town were under an interdict, the religious orders were not affected unless the interdict specifically included them.

²² *þe orisons whiche been songoun schul be songoun (schal be seyde) stondinge*. The words in brackets indicate the alternative practice: the orisons can either be sung or said.

²³ *Whan þe preface is seyde at masse*. The preface comes immediately

before the Sanctus in the Mass and begins 'Vere dignum et iustum est'. There are a number of Proper Prefaces for the several seasons.

²⁴ *þe Offertorie.* Immediately after the Creed the celebrant places the Elements on the Altar with accompanying prayers. This is known as the Offertory. At the end of the Offertory the celebrant turns to the people and begins the 'Orate, fratres'. Then follow the secret Prayers for the day, ending with ' Per omnia saecula saeculorum '.

²⁵ *þey schul dwelle greuelinge til ' Per omnia ' at ' Pax domini,'* i. e. they remain kneeling from the Sanctus throughout the Consecration and Elevation (' duringe þe leuacioun ') until after the celebrant has made the Fraction. He then says aloud ' Per omnia ', &c., and ' Pax Domini sit semper vobiscum '.

²⁶ *þe Post communions,* i. e. the Post-communion prayers for the day, said aloud by the Celebrant. They come at the end of the Mass, just before the ' Ite, missa est '.

²⁷ *In lentyn at þe verse of þe tracte.* During the Procession before the reading of the Gospel, the choir sing the Gradual for the day, consisting of a few verses of Holy Scripture. The Gradual is followed by the chant known as the Alleluia, but in penitential seasons instead of the Alleluia is sung the 'Tract', which consists of two or three verses of a Psalm. Le Brun explains the term Tract as something sung 'tractim', i.e. without break or interruption of other voices, by the cantor alone.

²⁸ *Preces of prime & of complyn.* The ' Preces ' begin with Kyrie, Pater, and Creed ; and continue with versicles, responsories, and the Confession, first of the Hebdomodarius and then of the people, with the Absolution. There is no Confiteor in the ' preces ' of Compline.

²⁹ *þe last verse saue one of Benedicite.* This verse is ' Benedicamus Patrem et Filium cum sancto Spiritu : laudemus et superexaltemus eum in saecula'.

³⁰ *Sequence.* A metrical composition which is sometimes attached to the Alleluia. An example of a Sequence is the *Dies Irae* of Thomas of Celano sung in Masses of the Dead.

³¹ *Half dobel Festis.* Seint Lucy (Virgin and Martyr, Dec. 13); Seint Nicholas (Bish. and Conf., Dec. 6); Fest of Innocentis (Dec. 28); Seint Thomas of Caunterbiri (Bish. and Mart., Dec. 29); þe vtas (octave) of Epiphanie (Jan. 13); Seint Anneys (Mother of Our Lady, July 26); Seint Agase (Virg. and Mart., Feb. 5); Holicrosse (Sept. 14); Apparicioun of Michel (Archangel, May 8); Octaue of Ascencioun (eighth day after Ascension); Octaue of Seint Antony (Abbot, Jan. 24); Octaue of seynt John Baptist (July 1); Seint Marie Magdalene (July 22); Translacioun of Seynt Thomas (i. e. of Canterbury, July 7); Seynt Margare (Virg. and Mart., July 20); vtas of Seint Laurence (Mart., Aug. 17); Seynt Lowis (Conf., his feast is Aug. 25, but does not generally have an octave ; probably his octave (Sept. 1) was observed at Longchamp on account of his connexion with that House); Decollacioun of Seint John (Aug. 29); vtas of Nativite of oure Ladi (Sept. 15); Seint Martin (Bish. and Conf., Nov. 11); Seynt Elizabeþ (? Queen of Lusitania, widow, July 8); Seynt Cecile (Virg. and Mart., Nov. 22); Seynt Katerin (Virg. and Mart., Nov. 25); vtas of Corporis Cristi (eight days after Thursday following Trinity Sunday).

³² *Festis douce dobles,* i. e. Feasts described in the Roman Kalendar as Duplex primae classis '.

³³ *Boþ of þe one euynsonge & of þe oþer.* All Double Feasts have two evensongs, i. e. their observance begins with the evensong of the evening before (known as 'first vespers'), while the evensong on the day itself is called 'second vespers'.

³⁴ *Festis doubles.* The first eight feasts named need no comment. Seint Antoun (Abbot, Jan. 17); Cathedra sancti Petri (it is doubtful whether Cathedra S. Petri Romae, Jan. 18, or Cathedra S. Petri Antiochiae, Feb. 22, is meant: both are 'Duplex majus'); Seint Mathee (Apos., Feb. 24); Seynt Gregori (presumably S. Gregory the Great, Pope and Conf., March 12); Seynt Benet (Abbot, Mar. 20); vtas of Seynt Barnabe (June 18); vtas of Seint Petir and Paule (July 6); Commemoracioun of Seynt Paule (June 30); Ad uincula Sancti Petri (MS. Sancte Petre, Aug. 1); Seynt Laurence (Mart., Aug. 10); Seint Clare (Virg., Aug. 12); Seint Lowis Bischopp (i. e. of Toulouse, Aug. 19); Seint Bartholemu (Apos., Aug. 24); Augustyn, doctor (Aug. 28); Seint Misshel (i. e. Dedicatio S. Michaelis Archangeli, Sept. 29); Seint Jerome (Pres. and Conf., Sept. 30); Translacioun of Seynt Lowis: no prescribed date for this: probably a local cult.

³⁵ *Asperges.* The short service before the Principal Mass when the celebrant makes a procession and sprinkles the holy water.

³⁶ *Whan þey sey many houres to gederis.* Sometimes several 'hours' were said one immediately after the other: this is sometimes called saying them 'by accumulation'.

³⁷ *Newme.* A term in mediaeval music theories denoting generally either a kind of melody or a notational sign. The *Catholic Encyclopaedia* describes it thus: 'Applied to a melody, the term means a series of tones sung without words, generally on the last vowel of a text. . . . The usual place of such neums is, in responsorial singing, especially at the end of the Alleluia which follows the Gradual of the Mass. In the later Middle Ages, however, from about the twelfth century onwards, the custom grew up of adding neums, definite formulae, one for each mode, to the office antiphons.' *Cath. Ency.* x, pp. 765-773 (H. Bewerunge).

³⁸ *þe blessinge of þe tabcl.* This is to some extent a repetition of what has already been prescribed earlier on fol. 79-81; but it is given more in detail here, and includes the special Benedictions for the chief Festivals.

³⁹ '*Miserere mei deus' wiþ alle þe versis,* i. e. the whole of the Miserere is said antiphonally.

⁴⁰ *Seyinge wiþ owte oremus.* The word 'Oremus' is omitted at this point before the 'Retribuere'.

⁴¹ *Schere þu, sday,* i. e. Maundy Thursday, the Thursday in Holy Week.

⁴² *Lowli & wiþowte ani more.* Breviary 'Totum secreto . . . sine pronuntiatione aliqua'.

⁴³ *þere as none estori shal be first entrid,* i. e. in which no 'history' shall be first entered, that is to say, in which the lesson is not the beginning of a historical book.

⁴⁴ *Seynt Siluester* (Pope and Conf., Dec. 31); Seynt Leon (Pope, Conf., and Doct., April 11); Seynt Eustache (i. e. SS. Eustace and his companions, Mart., Sept. 20).

⁴⁵ *Fest of translacioun of Seynt Frounceys,* May 25. The nominal date of the Translation was May 25, 1230, but it is practically certain that the actual

Translation of the Saint's remains to the church of San Francesco had been carried out by the Minister General, Elias of Cortona, several days earlier.

[46] *Grete antymes.* The so-called 'great Antiphons' are sung at Evensong before and after the Magnificat on the last eight days of Advent, that is from December 16 onwards. They were formerly called the O's, as each Antiphon began with the word O. The first of them, on Dec. 16, is 'O Sapiencia', and is so marked in the Kalendar.

GLOSSARY

[For *A Generall Rule to teche euery man that is willynge for to lerne to serve a lorde or mayster.*]

A

Amener, almoner, 13. 6.
Assay, the formal tasting of a dish by a servant, to see if it is poisoned, 14. 30.

C

Coster, a wall-hanging, 11. 6.

D

Dogdrawght, dogdrawe, an unknown fish, possibly cod, 17. 4.
Doucet, a sweet dish (see note), 17. 12.
Durmant, a fixed table, 13. 28.

E

Ewer, ewerer, the official in charge of arrangements for washing, 11. 22.
Ewry, the place where ewers, towels, etc., were stored, 11. 25.

H,

Hallyng, tapestry or painted cloth for a hall, 11. 5.
Herberoure, guest-master, entertiner, 15. 17.

K

Kynde, natural, proper, etc., 11. 6, etc.

L

Leche, slice, a dish consisting of sliced meat, 17. 15. (O. F. *lesche.*)
Lese þen, unless, 17. 12.
Leuereys, retainers, servants in livery, 11. 14.

P

Panter, the officer in charge of the pantry (originally 'baker'), 11. 21.
Pece, cup, 17. 20.

S

Sewe, serve, 12. 21.
Sewer, a sewer, waiter, 11. 24.
Sprottes, sprats, 17. 4.
Surnape, a second cloth laid on the table immediately before the lord, 13. 30.

T

Taill, tally, reckoning, 11. 14.
Take, deliver, 13. 13.
To, till, 12. 18.
Trenchour, trencher of bread (see note), 13. 4.

V

Vnto, until, 12. 5.
Voyder, tray for removing broken meats, etc., 13. 6.

W

Woke, week, 11. 15.

GLOSSARY

[For *The Thirde Order of Seynt Franceys* and *The Rewle of Sustris Menouresses enclosid*]

A

Algatis, in any case, 87. 16.
Alle Halwyn, All Saints, Allhallows, 86. 19.
Apostle, Pope, 89. 26.
Assentement, assent, agreement, 88. 31.
Assigned, transferred, removed, 87. 31.
Assoyle, absolve, 88. 21.
Assoylid, excused of, deprived of, 94. 16.
Atrete, slowly without break (=tractim), 104. 34.
Auenaunt, suitable, 103. 25.
Auenture, chance, 88. 23.
Avale, let down, 92. 7. [OF. avaler.]
Axen, demand, 94. 16.
Ayenst, against, 48. 25.

B

Besili, carefully, diligently, 54. 22.
Bigginge, buying, 96. 11. Sourfait of bigginge, excessive buying.
Bihote, promise, 83. 32.
Boundes, bands, sashes, 49. 13.
Brennyng, burning, 47. 13.
Brent, burnt, 94. 30.
Buystouse, rough, coarse, 84. 19.

C

Catallis, chattels, possessions, 96. 7.
Cawcion, bond, security, 48. 16.
Ceroferessis, acolyte, taperer, 108. 21.
Chausures, shoes, 85. 4.
Chesiple, chasuble, 91. 4.
Chesyn, choose, 95. 24.
Cierge, candle, 107. 24.
Clepid, called, 98. 12.
Clerete, honour, 90. 5.
Clogere, belfry, 104. 1.
Cloos, cloister, 104. 11.
Conge, leave, permission, 82. 15.
Congruertly, suitably, 52. 25.
Continementis, holdings, property, 81. 5.
Couenable, suitable, 82. 35.
Couent, convent, 82. 29, etc.

D

Decollacioun, beheading, 107. 32.
Demurid, demure, 84. 12.
Denounsid, reported, 98. 25.
Depart, bestow, impart, 47. 31.
Desseuerid, separated, 87. 25.
Disclawnder, slander, 90. 34.
Distreyne, constrain, compel, 100. 29.
Dortre, Dortoure, dormitory, 85. 7, etc.

E

Efformid, informed, 100. 13.
Enfayrid, adorned, 81. 11.
Enpeyre, injure, impair, 100. 2.
Ententifeliche, carefully, 87. 23.
Entredite, interdict, 105. 26.
Equypollent, of equal rank, 114. 18.
Esloignid, extended, protracted, 93. 32.
Estori, history, 113. 4.
Estreyteli, strictly, 89. 24.
Exchew, eschew, 52. 8.
Eyrin, eggs, 86. 25.

F

Familieres, members of the household, servants, 94. 17.
Fayrid, adorned, 81. 24.
Feri, an ordinary week-day (not a festival), 103. 15.
Fermeri, infirmary, 89. 20.
For as mochel, forasmuch, order that, 87. 25.
Forbarrid, forbidden, 89. 16.
Freytoure, refectory, 102. 22.

G

Gasingis, spectacles, 49. 18.
Goget, Guyches, wicket, grating, 91. 36. [Fr. guichet.]
Grayel, gradual, 107. 20.
Greuelinge, prostrate, 106. 8.
Greueninge, prostrate, 106. 9.

H

Halwid, consecrated, 114. 27.
Heilfully, in a wholesome or salutary way, 47. 26.

Glossary to the Thirde Order, and Sustris Menouresses 127

Hele, health, 86. 33.
Hende, gentle, gracious, 81. 10.
Heue, lift, 89. 2.
Holpyn, helped, 99. 6.
Houseled, communicated, 50. 35.

I
Importabel, unbearable, 100. 23.
Intrat, introit, 107. 1.
I-putte ouer, transposed, 113. 7.
Iuyelles, jewels, 99. 3.

J
Jangeling, disputing, 52. 10.

K
Kepe, care, 90. 31.

L
Leafull, lawful, 48. 31.
Lefolli, lawfully, 92. 3.
Legacioun, bequest, 99. 2.
Lentoun, Lent, 107. 1.
Leuacioun, elevation, 102. 19.
Leueli, with leave, 82. 30.
Listresse, woman-lector, reader, 110. 31.

M
Meke, humble, plain, 49. 4.
Menours, Meneres, Menouresses, Franciscan Friars or Clarisses, 81. 2, etc.
Meuabel, movable, 99. 30.
Mo, more, 110. 6.
Monestyn, admonish, exhort, 94. 7.
Mow, must, 84. 32.
Myngin, remember, 94. 10.

N
Nameli, especially, 87. 17.
Neforþat, nevertheless, 101. 4.
Noysed, rumoured, 48. 5.
Nyȝe, draw near to, 82. 5.

O
Obey, bow, 105. 9.
Obeyinge, bowing, doing obeisance, 104. 22.
Obite, death, 53. 19.
Ouereste cote, outermost garment, 84. 21.
Owers, hours, 51. 8.
Owte take, except, 86. 18.
Owtrage, superfluity, excess, 84. 17.

P
Pasche, Easter, 116. 21.
Pontificacion, papacy, 55. 16.
Possessioners, proprietors, 47. 27.

Promitte, promise, 48. 23.
Purposid, put forward, present, 93. 10.

R
Recordinge, remembrance, recollection, 81. 8. reddur.]
Reddure, strictness, 82. 1. [N. F.
Refestid, refreshed, 86. 8.
Refreytouresse, the sister in charge of the 'refrectorium' or refectory, 102. 32.
Reine, kingdom, 89. 30.
Remew, remove, 82. 30.
Repreue, reprove, 83. 27.
Repreueable, reprovable, 83. 28.
Reuestrid, arrayed, 91. 8.
Rihtwisnesse, righteousness, 93. 7.
Rowndid, cut round, 85. 22.

S
Sad, grave, 92. 13.
Sadli, seriously, 101. 30.
Schet, shut, 91. 36.
Schlugri, laziness, sloth, 86. 3.
Sege, place, seat, 107. 11.
Seint Croyse, Holy Cross, 104. 7.
Skerid, frightened, 86. 4.
Sogettis, subject, 95. 19.
Somenerere, Semenere, apparitor. 102. 35.
Stabelriche, constantly, 86. 1.
Stamyn, an open woollen fabric, 84. 15. [Fr. estamine.]
Stawnche, quench, 86. 5.
Stere, guide, direct, 52. 14, etc.
Storer, treasurer, 52. 25.
Suen, follow, 87. 30.

T
To-dite, dress, 86. 27.
Þorwe, through, 110. 15.
Treyne, pause, 104. 38.

V
Vtas, octave, 107. 31, etc.

W
Warnid, furnished, 94. 5.
Werre, war, 82. 23.
Wytt, know, 55. 12.

Y
Yȝen, eyes, 84. 25.
Ymage, crucifix, 103. 4.
Ympnis, hymns, 106. 33.

Ȝ
Ȝouin, given, 96. 33.

The manufacturer's authorised representative in the EU for product
safety is Oxford University Press España S.A. of El Parque Empresarial
San Fernando de Henares, Avenida de Castilla, 2 - 28830 Madrid
(www.oup.es/en or product.safety@oup.com). OUP España S.A. also acts
as importer into Spain of products made by the manufacturer.
Printed and bound by CPI Group (UK) Ltd, Croydon, CR0 4YY

20/03/2026

02075337-0013